ROAD TRIP

WALES

THE ULTIMATE GUIDE TO WALES...

ROBBIE ROAMS

ABOUT THE AUTHOR...

Rob Standley aka Robbie Roams is a collie dog lover, keen traveller and travel guide book writer. In 2022, Robbie released *'North Coast 500 – The Road Trip of a Lifetime '* the first of his *'No Fuss Travel Guides'* which quickly became an Amazon best seller. His writing style contrasts the typical *'travel guide'* and was summarised excellently by a recent Amazon review *'Useful information delivered in a style which you imagine might be someone talking to you over a few pints'*. As well as writing travel books, he records 'No Fuss' travel videos for his YouTube channel which provide tips, hacks and first hand experiences. He currently lives in Staffordshire, UK with his partner Jasmin, 2 collie dogs - Archie & Gem, his pet goose Uncle Waldo and pet duck Penelope.

Published by No Fuss Travel Guides | Second Edition
First published in Great Britain 2022
Copyright © Robert Standley 2022
Photographs © Robert Standley
Additional Photographs © Shutterstock

Robert Standley has asserted his right under the Copyright, Designs & Patents Act, 1988, to be identified as the Author of this work.

ROBBIE, GEM & ARCHIE
SOUTH STACK LIGHTHOUSE | ANGLESEY

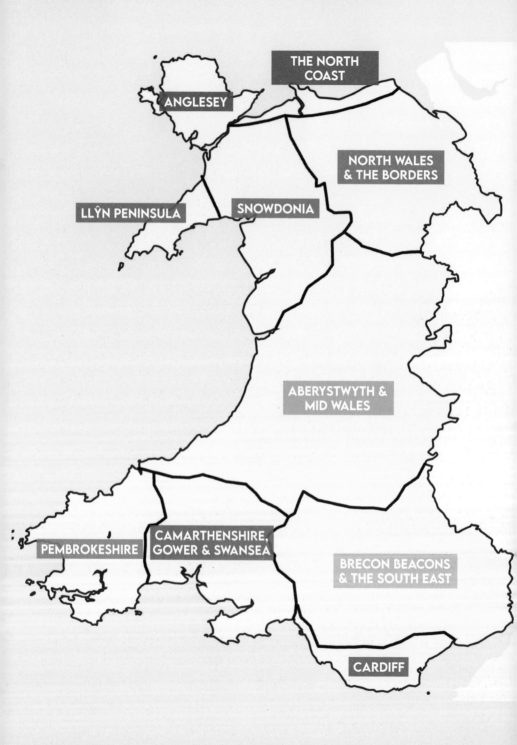

ROAD TRIP WALES

CONTENTS

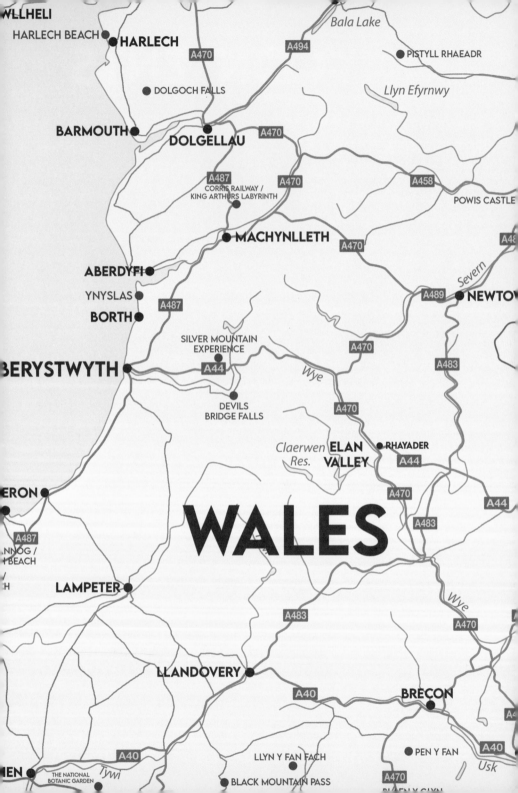

PLANNING YOUR ROAD TRIP

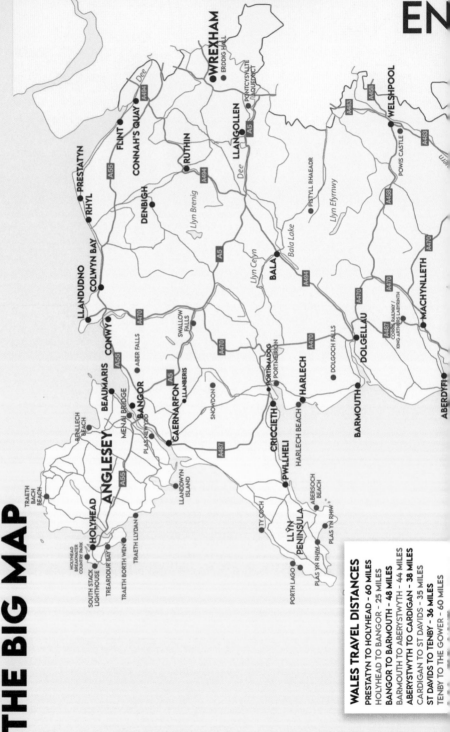

ROAD TRIP WALES
THE BIG MAP

EN

WREXHAM
ERDDIG HALL
PONTCYSYLLTE AQUEDUCT

WELSHPOOL
POWIS CASTLE

FLINT
CONNAH'S QUAY
PRESTATYN
RHYL
COLWYN BAY
LLANDUDNO

LLANGOLLEN
RUTHIN
DENBIGH

Llyn Brenig
Dee
Llyn Efyrnwy
PISTYLL RHAEADR

BALA
Bala Lake
Llyn Celyn

MACHYNLLETH
DOLGELLAU
CORRIS RAILWAY /
KING ARTHURS LABYRINTH
DOLGOCH FALLS

CONWY
ABER FALLS
SWALLOW FALLS
BEAUMARIS
MENAI BRIDGE
BANGOR
PLAS NEWYDD
LLANBERIS
CAERNARFON
SNOWDON

PORTHMADOG
PORTMEIRION
HARLECH
HARLECH BEACH

BARMOUTH

ABERDYFI

BENLLECH BEACH
ANGLESEY
TRAETH BACH BEACH
HOLYHEAD BREAKWATER COUNTRY PARK
HOLYHEAD
SOUTH STACK LIGHTHOUSE
TREARDDUR BAY
TRAETH BORTH WEN
TRAETH LLYDAN
LLANDDWYN ISLAND

CRICCIETH
PWLLHELI
ABERSOCH BEACH
TY COCH
LLŶN PENINSULA
PLAS YN RHIW
PLAS YN RHIW
PORTH LAGO

WALES TRAVEL DISTANCES
PRESTATYN TO HOLYHEAD - **60 MILES**
HOLYHEAD TO BANGOR - **25 MILES**
BANGOR TO BARMOUTH - **48 MILES**
BARMOUTH TO ABERYSTWYTH - **44 MILES**
ABERYSTWYTH TO CARDIGAN - **38 MILES**
CARDIGAN TO ST DAVIDS - **35 MILES**
ST DAVIDS TO TENBY - **36 MILES**
TENBY TO THE GOWER - **60 MILES**

A494, A55, A483, A458, A5, A470, A487

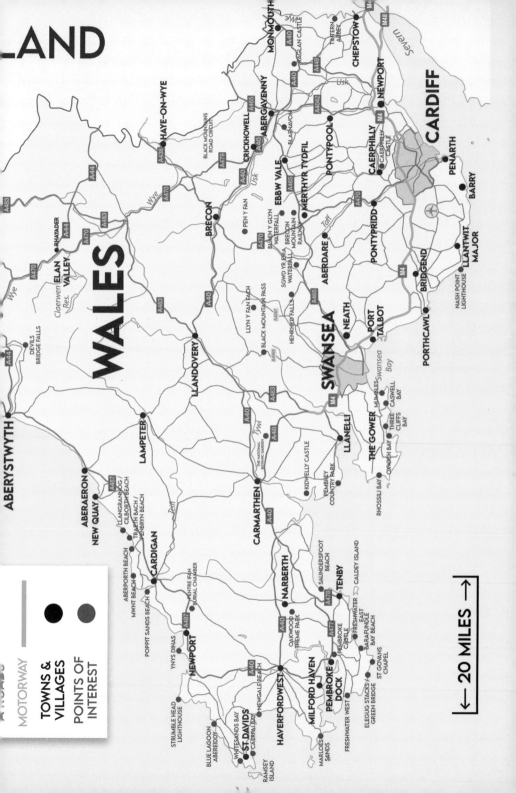

ROAD TRIPS IN WALES

SNOWDONIA NATIONAL PARK

THE UK'S BEST KEPT ROAD TRIP SECRET!

Vast mountainous landscapes, huge sweeping beaches and majestic medieval castles – a road trip in Wales has something for everyone. Now it might not be the largest country in the world but it certainly packs one hell of a punch! In terms of land area, it's actually similar to the Scottish Highlands, yet it has considerably more to see, do and experience.

Wales has a very well connected road system mainly made up of well maintained A roads allowing you to drive from location to location relatively quickly. There is the occasional single track road in rural areas, but these are generally few and far between.

There are an endless amount of routes to take and things to see which makes Wales an ideal road trip destination you can visit time and time again. From a weekend road trip around Anglesey to a full North to South coastal road trip, you really are spoilt for choice in this magical country!

It's no secret that people have been holidaying in Wales for centuries, however, road trips around the country go somewhat under the radar. The lure of the glossy and well promoted 'NC500' in Scotland is the first choice for many first time road trippers but in my honest opinion, Wales is the UK's best kept road trip secret!

I have fond childhood memories of visiting Aberystwyth in Mid Wales, where my sister and I would be shipped off to stay with my Grandparents at their static caravan every school holiday. From then I guess I've always had a real soft spot for Wales and I've been back many times since (mainly to North & Mid Wales), but, it wasn't until I started to visit and thoroughly research for this book that I realised what a sleeping giant this country is. In terms of road trip destinations, it is a dream.

So with all that said, what are you waiting for? Fasten your seatbelts and get ready for a road trip around one of the most magnificent places in the world!

I promise you, you are GOING TO LOVE IT!

Actually, hold on a second, there's a few things you need to do before you go! First of all, make sure you read this guidebook (don't forget to bring it with you on your road trip, it fits perfectly into a glovebox or in your back pack). I really have gone above and beyond to ensure you're armed with all the information and best locations to be able to plan your epic road trip. I always recommend that you thoroughly read the planning section where you'll get a better idea of what to expect and how to make a solid plan for your trip.

And with that in mind, let's get into planning your Welsh road trip adventure...

TOP TIP

ALWAYS REFER BACK TO THE WALES ROAD TRIP MAP ON PAGE 10!

HOW TO PLAN YOUR TRIP?

BUT FIRST, WHY YOU SHOULD PLAN...

In my opinion, planning is the bedrock to any epic road trip...
Just a little bit of effort in making a plan will save time, money and
stress which is a no brainer right? Significantly, you'll be guaranteed
to see all of the best sights and locations along the way. Imagine
getting home and realising you skipped the best beach in Wales
because you forgot to make a plan. Imagine getting home and your
kids are devastated that you didn't visit the mighty Welsh castle that
was at the top of their list. I think you probably get the picture now?
I'm really just trying to emphasise that making a plan, even a rough
one, will be 100% worth the short amount of time it takes to create.

I'm not saying a Welsh road trip can't be done on a wing and has to
be completely rigid, but, the whole purpose of your trip is to enjoy
yourself in this fantastic location. During the months of May, June, July
& August, Wales does get busy.

What does this mean? Well, it means that campsites, hotels, B&B's &
restaurants may be fully booked. It also means that the roads will be
busier = more time spent on the road = drives between places taking
longer than expected = a very stressful & less than ideal experience.

The point I'm making is don't stress yourself out **BY NOT
PLANNING AHEAD.** You want to fondly remember this journey
for all the right reasons, so don't let your lack of planning hold you
back. I do love a good old cliché and I used this Benjamin Franklin in
quote in my last guide book, *"If you fail to plan, you are planning to fail"*.

Now I've got that rant out of the way, let's put this book to use and
get planning!

TOP TIP

BRING THE GUIDEBOOK WITH YOU ON YOUR ROAD TRIP FOR REFERENCE!

HOW TO PLAN YOUR TRIP?

MAKING THE MOST OF THIS BOOK...

I've created this book in a logical way to help you maximise your Welsh Road trip. The book is divided into sections based on areas in Wales so you can dip in and out depending on how long your road trip is, or which specific areas you intend to visit.

PLEASE READ - I've compiled the areas into an order as though I was completing an anti-clockwise road trip starting in North Wales, following the coast around to the West and then heading South (the diagram below will give you a clearer idea of what I mean).

If you decide your road trip will be take more of a clockwise route, then perhaps plan your trip by reading the book from the back to the front?

Wales doesn't have a single set road trip like the NC500 in Scotland and this means you have more flexibility creating your own bespoke adventure. Alternatively, I have a fantastic set of road trip itineraries in this book that will point you in the right direction if that's something you'd prefer. The itineraries can be found from page 34.

ANTI-CLOCKWISE

PLEASE NOTE - THE GUIDE BOOK IS ORDERED IN AN ANTI-CLOCKWISE DIRECTION

GETTING TO WALES

TENBY

HOW TO GET THERE FROM WITHIN THE UK

DRIVING TO WALES

Wales is located to the west of England and can be easily accessed through the UK's motorway network. If you're coming from the North, the M6 will take you on to the M56 which links to the A55 North Wales Express Way. If you're coming from the South, the M5 links onto the M4 which will carry you across to South Wales. From the Midlands, you have multiple options depending on your road trip starting location.

DRIVE TIMES TO CARDIFF	DRIVE TIMES TO WREXHAM
London - 3 hr 13 min	London - 4 hr 5 min
Glasgow - 6 hr 30 min	Glasgow - 4 hr 10 min
Manchester - 3 hr 40 min	Manchester - 1 hr 15 min
Newcastle - 5 hr 30 min	Newcastle - 3 hr 44 min
Ipswich - 4 hr 13 min	Ipswich - 4 hr 10 min
Southampton - 2 hr 34 min	Southampton - 4 hr 10 min
Birmingham - 2 hr 20 min	Birmingham - 1 hr 40 min
Leeds - 4 hr 10 min	Leeds - 1 hr 57 min
Nottingham - 3 hr 10 min	Nottingham - 2 hr 10 min

TRAIN

Cardiff is a main train hub with services arriving to there from London and other UK cities. Some are direct into Cardiff, others will stop at Bath and a change may be required. In terms of North Wales, access to places such as Wrexham or Rhyl via train are made with a connection at Chester. Hiring a car is a straightforward option from Cardiff or Wrexham depending on your road trip direction.

CAR & PASSENGER FERRIES

Stenaline run a ferry service from Belfast to Liverpool which takes 8 hours with a stop on the Isle of Man with two sailings per day. Dublin may be a quicker option with the route to Holyhead in Anglesey taking 3 hours 30 minutes.

FLYING

Direct flights operate to Cardiff from both Belfast & Edinburgh. Flights are often less than £70 each way when booked in advance. Belfast even has flights cheaper than £40 each way if booking 2-3 months ahead. Bristol Airport is a short ride from Cardiff and has direct flights from Glasgow, Edinburgh, Newcastle & Belfast. Liverpool & Manchester airports are close to North Wales and may offer cheaper flights than Cardiff.

HOW TO GET THERE FROM OUTSIDE THE UK

FLYING

Cardiff has direct flights from Amsterdam, Dublin & Edinburgh which are major European hubs serving airports around the world. Alternatively, flying into Manchester or Liverpool (close to North Wales) could cut out the connecting flight to Cardiff.

FLIGHT TIMES TO CARDIFF	FLIGHT TIMES TO MANCHESTER
Edinburgh - 1 hr 20 min	New York - 8 hrs
Belfast - 1 hr 20 min	Los Angeles - 13 hrs
Amsterdam - 1 hr 15 min	Beijing - 12 hrs
Dublin - 1 hr	Rome - 2 hr 45 min

HOW LONG DO I NEED?

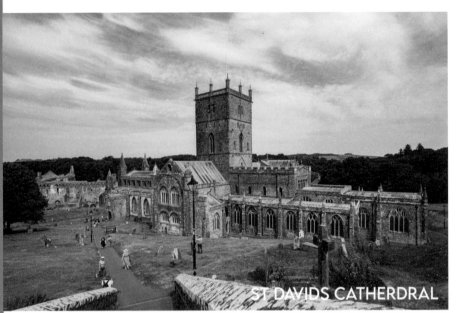

ST DAVIDS CATHERDRAL

LET'S TALK ABOUT TIME...

An important part of the planning process is deciding how long your Welsh road trip will take (or how much time you can get off work). Now the brilliant thing about Wales is that it has no set route! This flexibility means you can go for as long or as short a time as you like and even come back at a later date to visit new locations.

My suggested itineraries on page 34 feature a range of options including road trips lasting for a weekend, 5 days, 7 days, 10 days, 14 days and beyond! So don't stress, Wales is ready and waiting for you regardless of how long you have available...

A FEW ROAD TRIP EXAMPLES...

A Weekend in Anglesey - Weekend or 2 Nights
The Best of Snowdonia - Weekend or 2 Nights
Pembrokeshire & The South Coast - 5 Days
The Welsh Coast 400 North to South - 7 Days
The Complete Welsh Road Trip - 10 Days

GETTING AROUND WALES...

CAR, CAMPERVAN, CARAVAN OR MOTORBIKE?

There are obvious pros and cons to each method of transport. Cars are generally smaller and more nimble than a campervan or a car towing a caravan, making them easier to navigate car parks and roads along the way. Camping is still an option, but, you may limited on space for luggage and camping gear. As a result, hotels, B&B's and glamping locations will probably be more convenient.

Wales doesn't have quite as many precarious single track roads as other popular road trip destinations such as the Scottish Highlands. Therefore, you'll have less to worry about if you do bring your campervan or caravan. With an abundance of places to pull over, make a brew and enjoy the scenery – you'll be set for the road trip of a lifetime in your camper or caravan. Campsites are plentiful and excellently located all across Wales. I've included plenty of campsites throughout the book to make it easy for you.

Any keen motorbikers will already know what an epic destination Wales is to explore on two wheels. Twisting and turning mountain passes lead into huge open stretches of coastal road (sounds like a dream doesn't it?). Of course on a bike you'll be more nimble and able to cover the ground much quicker. You also have the option of camping or staying at hotels which is a win-win situation. Keep your eyes peeled for some of the terrific mountain passes and loops that I've included throughout the guide - these really are a motorbikers paradise. The Black Mountain Pass, Snowdon Loop and Gospel Pass are a few you don't want to miss out on.

TOP TIP

WHY NOT HIRE A CAMPERVAN FOR YOUR ROAD TRIP? 100% WORTH IT! QUIRKYCAMPERS.COM IS A GOOD PLACE TO START LOOKING...

HOW MUCH DOES IT COST?

The cost of your Wales road trip will vary depending on the length of time, type of accommodation and general day to day spending such as meals and gifts. Below are some rough expenses so you can work out a budget for your trip. Bear in mind these are just an average and your road trip can done for more or less depending on your budget.

STAYING AT CAMPSITES...

ITEM	DAILY COST	WEEKLY COST
Campsite Fees	£15-£25 depending on electric hook ups, extra cars etc.	£120
Fuel	£10-£20 per day depending on the fuel economy of your car or campervan and how far you are travelling.	£100
Food & Drink (Based on 2 People)	£20-£40 depending on meals out, coffee shops and self catering. There are great restaurants through-out Wales so don't miss out there.	£210
Activities	£15-£20 most of the locations are free but please factor in entry tickets to Castles, Museums or even some adrenaline fueled activities.	£120
Parking, Toilet Fees & Miscellaneous	£5-£7 - always bring spare change for parking, toilets and other miscellaneous items.	£40
Gifts & Souvenirs	£8-£10 depending on your preferences. There are some great gifts to pick up along the route!	£60
Weekly Total (Price for 2 people)		**£650**

CAMPERVAN HIRE

ITEM	DAILY COST	WEEKLY COST
Campervan Hire	£85-£150 depending on season and campervan type. Low season is generally cheaper.	£900

CAR HIRE

ITEM	DAILY COST	WEEKLY COST
Car Hire	£20-£40 per day depending on availability and which class of car you require. Premium / luxury cars will run beyond £40 per day.	£200

STAYING AT HOTELS AND B&B'S...

ITEM	DAILY COST	WEEKLY COST
Hotel or B&B Room	£50-£140 depending on time of year, availability and quality of the accommodation.	£500
Fuel	£10-£20 per day depending on the fuel economy of your car or campervan and how far you are travelling.	£100
Food & Drink (Based on 2 People)	£20-£40 depending on meals out, coffee shops and self catering. There are great restaurants through-out Wales so don't miss out there.	£210
Activities	£15-£20 most of the locations are free but please factor in entry tickets to Castles, Museums or even some adrenaline fueled activities.	£120
Parking, Toilet Fees & Miscellaneous	£5-£7 - always bring spare change for parking, toilets and other miscellaneous items.	£40
Gifts & Souvenirs	£8-£10 depending on your preferences. There are some great gifts to pick up along the route!	£60
	2 People Weekly Total	**£1030**

TOP TIP

IF HIRING A CAR OR CAMPERVAN, TAKE OUT 'CAR HIRE EXCESS INSURANCE' – IT COSTS AROUND £4 PER DAY AND IS MUCH BETTER VALUE THAN THE EXPENSIVE BOLT ONS THE CAR HIRE COMPANY WILL TRY AND SELL YOU. IT WILL ALSO SAVE YOU STRESSING ABOUT ANY POTENTIAL COLLISIONS OR DAMAGE. GOOGLE 'CAR HIRE EXCESS INSURANCE' THERE ARE MANY PROVIDERS.

WHEN SHOULD I VISIT WALES?

Wales is a country blessed with beauty regardless of the time of year. However, I've broken down the year into 3 specific periods to give you a better of idea of what to expect when you visit...

THE WINTER SEASON - NOVEMBER TO MARCH

PROS

• Roads are quiet – you won't come across much if any traffic especially in the rural parts of Wales. Tourism is at its lowest.
• Most of the fabulous beaches, castles and stops will be very quiet. You could even have some of them to yourself.
• Hotel / B&B availability is generally good. You may be able to grab some great deals on Air B&B's or Glamping sites.
• You may catch the last of the beautiful autumnal colours.
• You'll get great sunsets earlier in the day if the weather is nice, don't forget most of the Welsh coast gets amazing sunsets with its westerly location.
• No dog restrictions on beaches.

CONS

• The weather can be very cold, wet, windy & icy making for a less enjoyable experience.
• The days are much shorter with the sun setting as early as 4pm in the middle of December.
• Roads can become impassable due to snow and ice, this is quite rare and only applicable to rural / mountainous area.
• Some museums, castles & attractions are closed for the winter or have reduced opening times.
• Outdoor activities such as kayaking, hiking and excursions may not be running or available.
• Most campsites are closed throughout the winter period, some do still open but you need to check in advance of travelling.

TOP TIP

THE WINTER SEASON IS THE BEST TIME TO BAG A DEAL WITH HOTELS & AIR BNBS, ASK IF THEY DO ANY OFFERS!

THE SHOULDER SEASON – APRIL TO EARLY MAY & LATE SEPTEMBER TO OCTOBER

PROS

• Roads are quieter – you won't come across as much traffic throughout your trip.

• Most of the fabulous beaches, castles and stops will be very quiet. You could even have some of them to yourself.

• Hotel / B&B availability is generally good (always book ahead to be on the safe side).

• Campsite availability is generally good (always book ahead).

• You'll get great sunsets earlier in the day if the weather is nice, don't forget most the Welsh coast gets amazing sunsets with its westerly location.

• You'll see the iconic Daffodil bloom in the spring along with new born lambs (typically February and March).

• The Autumnal colours come to life in late September and October. Woodland areas will glow with warm amber tones.

CONS

• The weather can occasionally be very cold, wet, windy & icy making for a less enjoyable experience. Especially in the rural and mountainous areas.

• Roads should generally be fine but may be occasionally covered with snow, ice or flooded in rural areas.

• Most castles, museums and attractions are open but check ahead (some may close in November).

• Outdoor activities such as kayaking, hiking and excursions may not be limited or not available.

• Whilst availability at campsites, hotels may be good, some of them don't open until as late as April and can often close as early as October. Always check ahead in advance to avoid disappointment. Some campsites may open out of season just to accommodate you - it's always worth asking.

THE SUMMER SEASON – MID MAY TO MID SEPTEMBER

PROS

- Generally better weather with milder temperatures and less rain (although not guaranteed).
- All Hotels / B&B's are open (always book ahead).
- All campsites are open (always book ahead).
- All museums, castles & local attractions are open.
- Outdoor activities such as kayaking, hiking and excursions are fully running.
- You'll get great sunrises and sunsets if the weather is on your side. Don't forget most of the Welsh coast gets amazing sunsets with its westerly location.
- The days are long with sunsets as late as 9.45pm in June giving you plenty of time to explore and adventure.
- You can see specific wildlife such as puffins and other migrating birds.

CONS

- The roads are at their busiest and you can be stuck behind multiple vehicles along the route (more tourists, caravans and motorbikers).
- Hotels / B&B's may be booked up weeks if not months in advance during this season and can often be more expensive .
- Campsites may booked up weeks if not months in advance (always try and book ahead).
- Beaches, castles and attractions will be at their busiest. Railway attractions will require bookings a few days in advance.
- You may struggle to find parking at beaches and the most popular destinations.
- There may be longer waits in supermarkets, shops and local restaurants.
- Some beaches have dog restrictions during this period.

TOP TIP

AVOID THE SCHOOL HOLIDAYS AT THE END OF JULY AND THE WHOLE OF AUGUST IF POSSIBLE. IT WILL BE QUIETER WHILST STILL POTENTIALLY HAVING GOOD WEATHER!

MWNT BEACH - CEREDIGION

ACCOMMODATION

CAMPSITES

There are a couple of ways to approach your accommodation. The first option is camping! There are many campsites in superb locations across the whole of Wales. Most campsites have top facilities and electric hook ups should you need it. Camping allows you slightly more freedom, especially if you're doing the route in something like a campervan, motorhome or caravan. The cost to stay at each campsite is also a lot less than most hotels and B&B's, but you do have to factor in the cost of the campervan or camping equipment.

Throughout this guidebook I've listed many great campsites in each area of Wales, but don't use this as gospel, there are plenty more out there if you Google hard enough. With all campsites, I would highly recommend booking ahead or double checking they will be open when you plan to visit.

MY CAMSPITE TOP PICKS...

LLYN GWYNANT CAMPSITE - SNOWDONIA | SHELL ISLAND - LLANBEDR | LLEITHYR FARM HOLIDAY PARK - ST DAVIDS | THREE CLIFFS BAY HOLIDAY PARK - GOWER | CARDIFF CAMPING PARK

SHELL ISLAND CAMPSITE

ACCOMMODATION

HOTELS, B&B'S AND GLAMPING

If you're simply not a fan of camping, Wales is packed full of fantastic hotels, B&B's, cottages and glamping pods. Prices can often be more expensive in the summer season and availability is patchy unless you book ahead. As with the campsites, I've listed some of my favorite hotels & B&B's throughout the guidebook, but, if you're struggling to find space there are plenty more out there. I would recommend using Booking.com, Airbnb and Google to find alternative digs!

Staying in a cottage, quirky Airbnb or glamping pod can really make your road trip special. Wales has a wealth of these kind of places so start thinking outside the box to spice up your options. We like to have a few nights camping and then spend a night or two in a hotel or quirky cabin just to get the best of both worlds. Maybe this could work for you too?

MY HOTEL & B&B TOP PICKS...

TREARDDUR BAY HOTEL - ANGLESEY | BRYN DINAS PODS - SNOWDONIA | TWR Y FELIN HOTEL - ST DAVIDS | SPILMAN HOTEL - CAMARTHEN | VOCCO ST DAVIDS - CARDIFF

HOW MUCH DO CAMPSITES & HOTELS COST?

Campsite costs vary depending on the size of your camper, caravan motorhome or if you're camping in a tent. Below are a few examples...

Motorhome - £20.50 | Motorhome over 8m - £26 | Car & Tent - £20.50 Motorbike & Tent - £18.00 | Electric Hook Up - £6.00 | Awning - £6.00

Hotel prices can vary depending on the season and Airbnb's or glamping pods may require 2 night bookings in the busy months. Expect to pay between £50-£140 per night on average.

 ROBBIEROAMS.COM

PACKING FOR YOUR TRIP

WHAT SHOULD YOU BRING WITH YOU?

Most of this is common sense, but, take a read just in case you've forgotten something obvious. I haven't listed things like underwear because frankly, some people don't even wear it. Like most of the UK, the weather in Wales can change in a heartbeat. Being prepared for all eventualities will ensure your trip is as enjoyable as possible.

CLOTHING ESSENTIALS

- **Waterproof / Windproof Jacket** – essential in Wales.
- **Winter Coat** – waterproof options are better (you might not need this in summer).
- **Fleeces / Jumpers** – anything you can layer up when it gets chilly.
- **Warm Trousers** – potentially think about a waterproof option.
- **Warm Socks** – you might need a few pairs to rotate if they get wet.
- **Scarf, Hat & Gloves** – depending on the time of year these are life savers!
- **Swimwear** – if you're brave enough to take a dip in those wonderful Welsh waters? The beaches are so inviting!
- **Walking Boots** – paths are often muddy, wet or uneven. Bring a carrier bag or something to put them in to stop mud from getting in your car or van. You'll thank me later for this one.
- **Trainers or Flip Flops** – for relaxed use in the car, van or around the town. Remember there's gonna be some long drives!
- **Something for the evening** – perhaps you might want to put on something a little less outdoors'y if you're heading out for dinner or a few evening drinks?

TOILETRY & MEDICAL ESSENTIALS

- **Toilet Roll** – take at least a roll just in case.
- **Wet Wipes** – useful for a lot of things (bits and pits).
- **Sun Cream** – yes Wales does get sun!
- **Vaseline or Chapstick** – the wind can be cruel to your lips.
- **Paracetamol / Ibuprofen** – self-explanatory.
- **Small First Aid Kit** – at least a few plasters and anti-septic wipes.

- **Antihistamine Tablets** – you could be bitten by midges, ticks and all sorts - these may be your best friend.
- **Tick Comb** – essential if you're bringing your dog!
- **Dog Poo Bags** – same as above.

GADGET ESSENTIALS

- **Smartphone & Charging Cable** – always ideal for taking photos and videos! Also for using Google Maps offline. You can always charge whilst driving too if you have a 12v adaptor or in car USB port.
- **Camera** – not essential if you have a mobile phone but you'll certainly want to take some snaps along the way! Bring wide lenses.
- **Headlamp / Torch** – take one and leave it in the glovebox just to be on the safe side?
- **Sat Nav** – not necessary if you have a smartphone with Google Maps but some people prefer them. Don't always depend on them, sometimes the quickest route isn't the best route!
- **Power Bank** – in case you can't charge your devices through your car or campervan and you need some extra juice.

CAMPING & CAMPERVAN ESSENTIALS

- **Hoses, Universal Adaptors & Electric Cables** – essential to get water on campsites and refill points. Think about electric too.
- **Levelling Chocks** – if you're in a campervan, not all sites are flat.
- **Spare Gas Canisters** – useful but widely available in Wales.
- **Earplugs & Blindfold** – handy for camping.
- **Windbreak** – offers privacy and can be used on the beach too.
- **Warm Sleeping Bag or Bedding** – to keep you warm.
- **Dry Bag** – keep your important items in here if you're in a tent.
- **Multi Tool / Pen Knife** – we needed one of these multiple times.
- **Hot Water Bottle** – great to pop in your sleeping bag.
- **Micro Fibre Travel Towels** – what an invention these are!
- **Power Bank** – in case you can't charge your devices through your car or campervan, and you need some extra juice.
- **Headlamp / Torch** – a camping must have!
- **Wales Guide Book** – you own a decent one, why not bring it with you for some tips and light reading before bed?

▶ YouTube @ROBBIEROAMS

BRINGING YOUR DOG

GEM & JAS IN TENBY

IS WALES DOG FRIENDLY?

Absolutely! Bring your four legged friend/s along on the road trip and I can assure you they'll have as much fun as you. We took both of our border collies, Archie & Gem, on the Welsh Coast 400 trip in July 2022 and they had a blast. From having a cheeky pint at a pub to swimming in the sea, the dogs didn't get left behind at any point.

The majority of beaches, walks and castles are dog friendly. Some locations will ask for the dog to be kept on a lead and obviously any dog mess cleaned up. Some beaches do have restrictions from May to September but most still have a dog friendly section. Even most of the railway attractions are dog friendly.

Be sensible and follow any dog related signage and you'll be just fine. Always remember to keep dogs on leads around livestock and sheep. Most campsites allow dogs and more and more hotels now allow them. Always check ahead. Don't forget to bring a tick comb with you, have plenty of water available for them and do your best to keep them cool if the temperature begins to rise.

LEAVE IT NICER

On your road trip, please do your best to 'leave it nicer'. That means not making any mess, being kind and respectful, sticking to the designated paths and roads, emptying grey waste and chemical loos in the correct place, buying and eating locally to help the local economy and generally being a good human being.

Unfortunately, a small minority of people give people like us (road trip lovers, adventurers and tourists) a bad name by leaving rubbish (including human waste), lighting fires in places that significantly damage the habitat and being verbally and physically abusive to other people.

The danger is that this minority spoil it for everyone!

Please do your bit along the way. From my experience, the people in Wales are incredibly friendly, willing to help and give the warmest of welcomes so let's keep it that way!

Leave it nicer...

ABERYSTWYTH

PRIORITISING LOCATIONS

SNOWDON MOUNTAIN RAILWAY

PRIORITISE PLACES & THINGS YOU WANT TO SEE...

Wales is full of magnificent sights and a hell of a lot of things to do. Therefore, do your research, read this guidebook, check out Youtube or Instagram and physically write down a list of the main things you really want to see. I'd advise doing this for a couple of reasons…

1. By prioritising and making this list you'll ensure you see the places and things that are of most interest to you. You don't want to get home and realise you forgot to visit the best fish & chip shop in Wales or you missed one of the beast beaches. (Instagram is great for searching locations and cool photo ops).

2. It'll help you plan your route and make it easier to find suitable accommodation nearby.

Fortunately, you were smart enough to buy this guidebook where I've done most of the hard work for you. Each area of the Wales is broken down with a list of things to see and do in geographical order if you're heading anti-clockwise starting in North Wales.

EXAMPLE LIST OF LOCATIONS & SIGHTS...

PONCYSYLLTE AQUEDUCT

LLANDUDNO

CONWY CASTLE

MENAI SUSPENSION

LLANDDWYN ISLAND

SOUTH STACK LIGHTHOUSE

BEAUMARIS CASTLE

TY COCH

HELLS MOUTH

SNOWDON

ABER FALLS

PISTYLL RHAEADR

PORT MERION

BARMOUTH

ABERYSTWYTH

NEW QUAY

MWNT BEACH

STRUMBLE HEAD

BLUE LAGOON

ST DAVIDS

PEMBROKE CASTLE

FRESHWATER WEST

BARAFUNDLE BAY

TENBY

THE GOWER PENINSULA

CARDIFF

SWANSEA & THE MUMBLES

BRECON BEACONS

FIND ACCOMMODATION TO MATCH YOUR ROUTE

This might seem like common sense but it has to be said. Once you've got a list of the places you'd like to see, start penciling in some campsites or hotels near to them. Make sure your chosen accommodation fits in with your route. Use Google Maps to double check it's near the locations you are going to stop at and try and avoid going back on yourself or making unnecessary journeys.

TOP TIP

DOWNLOAD GOOGLE MAPS FOR OFFLINE USE!

DOWNLOAD THE WHOLE OF WALES FOR OFFLINE USE. YOU CAN DO THIS WITHIN THE GOOGLE MAPS APP AND IT ALLOWS YOU TO USE MAPS EVEN WHEN YOU DON'T HAVE PHONE SIGNAL! TRUST ME, GOOGLE MAPS WORKS WAY BETTER THAN APPLE MAPS FOR WALES. MOST POINTS OF INTEREST ARE LISTED ON GOOGLE MAPS TOO WHICH WILL SAVE YOU TIME & ISSUES!

ITINERARIES

ALWAYS WRITE DOWN YOUR ITINERARY...

And by this, I mean physically write down a plan for each day with pen and paper. Make sure to write down details on exactly where you are going to visit, where you are going to stay and use Google maps to get a rough idea of how long the drive is going to take each day. You could even think about restaurants, toilet stop offs and downtime if you really want to go into detail.

Google Maps is your best friend when making your plan, you can add multiple stops which will give you accurate journey times and show you if you're doubling back on yourself. If you're struggling for paper or need a template to work with, head to the back of the guidebook where I've created blank itinerary templates for you to write down your plan and keep it with you throughout your trip! There's also a journal / notes section.

SUGGESTED ITINERARIES...

So here are a few itineraries I've created that you might just like! Feel free to follow them exactly as they are or amend them and add in places as you wish. Remember, the whole point of this guidebook is to make your trip hassle free (or as hassle free as possible).

In this book I've broken down each area of Wales and provided you with the best places to see so you can easily create your own itinerary.

TOP TIP 👍

DON'T FORGET IT'S AN ADVENTURE!

JUST BECAUSE YOU'VE MADE AN ITINERARY DOESN'T MEAN YOU ALWAYS HAVE TO STICK TO IT. WALES IS GREAT TO EXPLORE! SO GO OFF THE BEATEN TRACK AND SEE WHAT HIDDEN GEMS YOU CAN FIND. IF YOU GET LOST I'M SURE THERE WILL BE A FRIENDLY LOCAL OR FELLOW EXPLORER WILLING TO HELP!

WELSH COAST 400 NORTH TO SOUTH 7 DAYS

A fantastic 7 day trip spanning 400 miles that takes in the best that Wales has to offer. From huge mountains to some of the greatest beaches in the world. This route has something for everyone and is perfect for a 1 week road trip. Don't forget you can do this in reverse if you start in the South. The accommodation is based on campsites so swap these out if you prefer hotels or B&B's.

DAY	JOURNEY	ACTIVITIES	ACCOMMODATION	DRIVE TIME
1	Llandudno to Snowdonia	LLandudno, Conwy Castle, Aber Falls, Rhaeadr Ewynnol Swallow Falls Waterfall.	Llyn Gwynant Campsite	1hr 50 mins
2	Snowdonia to Shell Island	Snowdon Watkin Pass Waterfall Hike, Portmeirion, Harlech Castle.	Shell Island Campsite	1hr 12 mins
3	Shell Island to Aberystwyth	Barmouth, Ynyslas, Aberystwyth Town, Mountain Railway, Fish & Chips.	Midfield Holiday Park	1hr 50 mins
4	Aberystwyth to St Davids	Aberaeron, New Quay, Mwnt Beach, Strumble Head Lighthouse, Blue Lagoon.	Lleithyr Farm Holiday Park	3hrs 20 mins
5	St Davids to Tenby	St Davids, Pembroke Castle, Freshwater West Beach, Elegug Stacks, St Govans Chapel, Barafundle Bay.	Penally Court Farm	2hrs 20 mins
6	Tenby to Gower Peninsula	Tenby, St Catherine's Island, Rhossili Bay, Oxwich Bay, Three Cliffs Bay, The Mumbles.	Three Cliffs Bay Holiday Park	2hrs 30mins
7	Gower Peninsula to Brecons	Cardiff, Black Mountains Road Circuit, Brecon, Pen Y Fan Walk.	Cefn Cantref Campsite or drive home.	3hrs 20mins

PEMBROKESHIRE & THE SOUTH COAST - 5 DAYS

5 days of Welsh coastal bliss! This is an ideal Monday-Friday trip where you will explore the stunning Pembrokeshire coast in detail from its magnificent beaches to its majestic medieval castles! This can be turned into a loop including the Brecon Beacons depending on your start point and end point. Feel free to add in your preferred stop offs.

DAY	JOURNEY	ACTIVITIES	ACCOMMODATION	DRIVE TIME
1	Cardiff to Gower Peninsula	Cardiff, Nash Point Lighthouse, Porthcawl Rest Bay Beach, Mumbles.	Three Cliffs Bay Holiday Park	1hr 57 mins
2	Gower Peninsula to Tenby	Three Cliffs Bay, Oxwich Bay, Rhossili Bay, Cefn Sidan Beach & Pembrey Country Park.	Penally Court Farm	2hrs 37 mins
3	Tenby to Milford Haven	Tenby, St Catherine's Island, Barafundle Bay. St Govans Chapel, Elegug Stacks, Freshwater West, Pembroke Castle	Sandy Haven Camping	1hr 50 mins
4	Milford Haven to Fishguard	Newgale Beach, St Davids, Whitesands Bay, Blue Lagoon, Strumble Head Light House.	Fishguard Bay Resort	2hrs 12 mins
5	Fishguard to Swansea	Ynys Dinas Walk, Pentre Ifan Burial Chamber, National Botanic Gardens, Swansea.	Riverside Holiday Park or return home	2hrs 9 mins

OPTIONAL DETOUR

BRECON BEACONS MOUNTAIN PASS

INSTEAD OF HEADING DIRECT TO SWANSEA, GO TO BONT FAWR AND THEN HEAD SOUTH THROUGH THE BLACK MOUNTAIN PASS TO UPPER BRYNAMMAN. THIS ROAD IS ONE OF THE BEST IN WALES AND BECAME POPULAR YEARS AGO AFTER BEING FEATURED ON AN EPISODE OF TOP GEAR! THE ROUTE WILL ADD ON AROUND 1 HOUR TO YOUR JOURNEY BUT IT WILL BE WORTH IT!

BARAFUNDLE BAY BEACH

THE COMPLETE WELSH ROAD TRIP - 10 DAYS

If time is on your side, this is the mother of all road trips in Wales! You will conquer all regions and drive away having experienced a lot that mighty Wales has to offer. This trip is planned in an anti-clockwise direction but can be done the opposite way. Don't forget to change out campsites to hotels or B&B's if that's your thing.

DAY	JOURNEY	ACTIVITIES	ACCOMMODATION	DRIVE TIME
1	Welshpool to Conwy	Powis Castle, Pontcysyllte Aqueduct, Llangollen, Llandudno, Conwy & Castle.	Conwy Holiday Park	2hrs 30 mins
2	Conwy to Anglesey	Aber Falls, Menai Bridge, Beaumaris & Castle, Benllech Beach, Cemaes Bay.	Pen Y Bont Campsite	2hrs 24 mins
3	Anglesey to Shell Island	South Stack Lighthouse, Trearddur Bay, Llanddwyn Island, Portmeirion, Harlech Castle, Shell Island.	Shell Island Campsite	3hrs 5 mins
4	Shell Island to Aberystwyth	Barmouth, Ynyslas, Aberystwyth Town, Mountain Railway, Fish & Chips.	Midfield Holiday Park	1hr 50 mins
5	Aberystwyth to St Davids	Aberaeron, New Quay, Mwnt Beach, Strumble Head Lighthouse, Blue Lagoon.	Lleithyr Farm Holiday Park	3hrs 20 mins
6	St Davids to Tenby	St Davids, Pembroke Castle, Freshwater West Beach, Elegug Stacks, St Govans Chapel, Barafundle Bay.	Penally Court Farm	2hrs 20 mins
7	Tenby to Gower Peninsula	Tenby, St Catherine's Island, Rhossili Bay, Oxwich Bay, Three Cliffs Bay, The Mumbles.	Three Cliffs Bay Holiday Park	2hrs 30mins

DAY	JOURNEY	ACTIVITIES	ACCOMMODATION	DRIVE TIME
8	Gower Peninsula to Cardiff	Swansea, Porthcawl, Nash-point Lighthouse, Barry Island, Cardiff.	Cardiff Caravan and Camping Park	2hrs 20 mins
9	Cardiff to Brecon Beacons	Cardiff, Black Mountains Road Circuit, Brecon, Pen Y Fan Walk.	Cefn Cantref Campsite	2hrs 40 mins
10	Brecon Beacons to Elan Valley	Gigrin Farm Red Kite Feeding Centre, Elan Valley Trail, Garreg Ddu Dam.	Elan Oaks - Camping & Caravan Site or return home	1hr 6 mins

TOP TIP

MIX UP YOUR ACCOMMODATION!

LONGER ROAD TRIPS CAN BE TEDIOUS IF YOU ARE CAMPING FOR THE ENTIRE DURATION. WHY NOT CONSIDER HAVING 1 OR 2 NIGHTS STAYING IN A HOTEL, AIRBNB OR GLAMPING LODGE WHERE YOU'LL HAVE A BIT MORE LUXURY, SPACE AND MORE PRIVATE FACILITIES? I ALWAYS LIKE TO ENJOY THE BEST OF BOTH WORLDS WHERE POSSIBLE, ESPECIALLY ON TRIPS OF 7-14 DAYS!

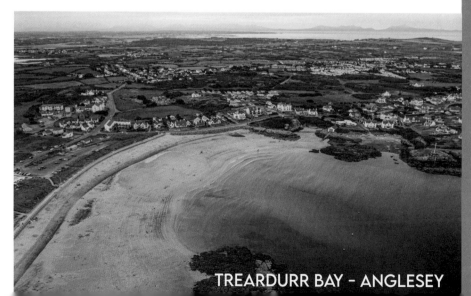

TREARDURR BAY - ANGLESEY

A WEEKEND IN ANGLESEY - 2 DAYS

Anglesey is truly amazing! 2 days and 2 nights here will be plenty for a short adventure where you'll take in jaw dropping scenery, ancient castles and wild beaches that could easily rival any in the UK! This trip is perfect for a weekend away or perhaps could be bolted on to one of the other itineraries. If you arrive on a Friday evening just book into a campsite or hotel nearby (ideally towards the south of Anglesey if you're following the itinerary).

DAY	JOURNEY	ACTIVITIES	ACCOMMODATION	DRIVE TIME
1	Beaumaris to Pen Y Bont	Menai Suspension Bridge, Plas Newydd House, Beaumaris & Castle, Benllech Beach, Cemaes Bay.	Pen Y Bont Campsite	1hrs 30 mins
2	Pen Y Bont	Holyhead Breakwater Country Park, South Stack Lighthouse, Trearddur Bay, Llanddwyn Island.	Awelfryn Campsite	1hrs 43 mins

TOP TIP 👍

WALK TO LLANDDWYN ISLAND!

A BEAUTIFUL 4 MILE THERE AND BACK WALK - YOU MUST DO IT.

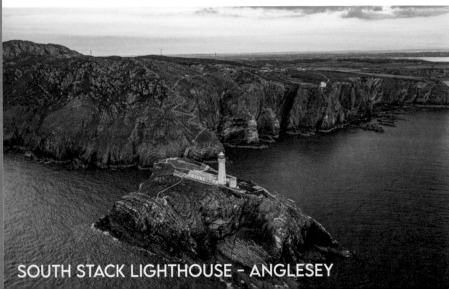

SOUTH STACK LIGHTHOUSE - ANGLESEY

BEST OF SNOWDONIA - 2 DAYS

The breathtaking Snowdonia National Park home of the mighty Snowdon - the highest mountain in Wales. A weekend or two night stay here will offer you the chance to explore rugged mountain landscapes, spectacular waterfalls and epic castles. The route begins in Conwy so if you arrive on a Friday evening and intend to follow the itinerary, aim to stay in a campsite or hotel nearby.

DAY	JOURNEY	ACTIVITIES	ACCOMMODATION	DRIVE TIME
1	Cowny to Llanberis	Conwy, Conwy Castle, Aber Falls, Llanberis, National Slate Museum, Snowdon Mountain Railway (Afternoon Booking), Llanberis Pass.	Llyn Gwynant Campsite	1hrs 30 mins
2	Llanberis to Betws-y-Coed	Portmeirion or Porthmadog, Harlech Castle, Harlech Beach, Betws-y-Coed, Rhaeadr Ewynnol Swallow Falls Waterfall.	Dolgam Campsite	1hrs 40 mins

LOOKING FOR ADRENALINE?

VISIT ZIP WORLD!
HIGHLY RECOMMENDED! CHECK OUT THE VELOCITY 2 ZIPLINE!

SNOWDON - SNOWDONIA

A WEEKEND IN THE BRECON BEACONS - 2 DAYS

Some of the finest mountains and countryside that Wales has to offer. The Brecon Beacons are a paradise for outdoor lovers and those that enjoy stunning scenery. The road trip will you see drive two of the UK's best mountain passes, explore beautiful waterfalls and visit charming Welsh towns, You're in for a real treat with this epic road trip!

DAY	JOURNEY	ACTIVITIES	ACCOMMODATION	DRIVE TIME
1	Abergavenny to Pen Y Pass	Gospel Pass (Black Mountains Circuit), Hay-on-Wye, Brecon, Pen-y-Fan, Sgwd yr Eira Waterfall.	Grawen Caravan & Camping Park	2hrs 20 mins
2	Pen Y Bont	Henryd Falls, National Showcaves Centre, Llyn y Fan Fach, Black Mountain Pass.	Brynglas Retreat Campervan Campsite	2hrs 24 mins

LOOKING FOR ADRENALINE?

CHECK OUT BLACK MOUNTAIN ADVENTURES

FANTASTIC OUTDOOR ACTIVITIES CENTRE INCLUDING KAYAKING, CLAY PIGEON SHOOTING, CAVING & MORE. I RECOMMEND THEM!

PEN Y FAN - BRECON BEACONS

ROAD TRIP TOP TIPS

Stay calm behind the wheel! Take your time, use passing places to let others overtake should you need to. The roads in Wales are generally very good so just enjoy the ride.

Create a killer playlist! You're gonna be spending a lot of time on the road and there's no better way to supplement the journey than with a great playlist! If you're using Spotify or something similar, make sure to download the songs for offline use, the signal around Wales can be hit and miss. If you're old school, just bring some CD's.

Don't forget it's an adventure! Just because you have an itinerary doesn't mean you always have to stick to it. Wales is perfect to explore so go off the beaten track and see what hidden gems you can find.

Stock up on essentials - Don't run out of fuel, water and essential supplies. Petrol stations are plentiful apart from in the rural areas.

Know your limits - don't overdo it! Set yourself a daily driving limit, give yourself chance to relax and actually enjoy the journey! Take breaks and swap drivers? Remember not to cram too much into each day.

Pack carefully - think about the weather! Cover all eventualities including rain, sun, wind and cold weather.

Download Google Maps offline - this one's essential! Download the whole of Wales for offline use. You can do this within the Google Maps app and it allows you to use maps even when you don't have phone signal! Trust me, Google Maps works way better than Apple Maps for navigation around Wales.

Book ahead - Yep there he goes again about planning and booking ahead. I told you once, I told you twice now here I am for a third time. Make sure you plan and book ahead, alright?

@ROBBIEROAMS

5 OF THE BEST BEACHES...

BARAFUNDLE BAY - PEMBROKESHIRE

A beautiful sandy bay backed by dunes and pine trees. Voted many times as one of the best beaches in the UK! Requires a half mile walk from Stackpole Quay car park, 100% worth it if you are mobile.

MWNT - CEREDIGION

A truly beautiful hidden cove on the Ceredigion coast! This place made my jaw drop and if you decide to visit here, you'll see the reason why! This blue flag beach has a seasonal take away café and is one of the best places for dolphin spotting. The views from the top of the hill are magnificent if you don't fancy the steep walk down to the beach itself.

HARLECH BEACH - SNOWDONIA

This beach is a jaw dropper! Flat white sand, stunning dunes and it's a long one (stretching for 4 miles). If you're heading North on the A496 you'll get a magnificent view right over the beach.

FRESHWATER WEST - PEMBROKESHIRE

The best place for surfing in Pembrokeshire! This wild & sandy paradise has limited free parking and Harry Potter Fans can spot Dobby's grave! RIP Dobby!

RHOSSILI BAY - GOWER PENINUSLA

The supermodel of British beaches! If I could choose one beach in the whole of Wales to visit, I think it would be this one! What a magnificent place.

5 OF THE BEST HIKES...

SNOWDON - SNOWDONIA

The highest mountain in Wales standing at a whopping 1,085 metres. With six main walking paths up and down the mountain, Snowdon is one of the UK's most popular mountain climbs and is no mean feat.

LLANDDWYN ISLAND - ANGLESEY

Park at the Newborough Forest car park (which has great facilities) and make the 1.5 mile walk either through the lush forest or along the beach to the stunning Llanddwyn Island. Try and avoid high tide when the island is cut off from the mainland and remember that this place is very exposed to the elements.

PEN Y FAN - BRECON BEACONS

The highest peak in South Wales! The 4 mile circular walk from the Storey Arms Outdoor Centre is the most popular route up and is achievable even for those that aren't in the best shape, great views!

DINAS ISLAND - PEMBROKESHIRE

A spectacular circular coastal walk which isn't a particularly long one at 3 miles but requires a moderate level of fitness. Expect hidden coves and epic headland.

FOUR WATERFALLS HIKE - BRECON BEACONS

Beautiful 4.5 mile walk accessed by the car park at Cwm Porth (£4 for the day) leading to 4 jaw dropping waterfalls. Get your camera ready!

5 OF THE BEST TOWNS & CITIES...

LLANDUDNO & CONWY - NORTH WALES

Quintessential Welsh Victorian seaside town which packs a punch. Conwy has a little bit of something for everyone and is a world heritage site home to the thirteenth-century 'Conwy Castle'.

ABERYSTWYTH - MID WALES

A university seaside town in Ceredigion, Aberystwyth is a must visit west coast location! A trip up Constitution Hill via the Cliff Railway will provide great views across the town. Fish and chips is a must from either the Pier or the chippy opposite! The town centre has a wealth of good shops, cafes, pubs and restaurants.

CARDIFF - SOUTH WALES

The capital and largest city in Wales! Cardiff seems to tick all boxes from castles to culture and watersports to pubs! Within 1 mile of the city centre, Cardiff has pretty much everything you can think of.

TENBY - PEMBROKESHIRE

Iconic picturesque sea side town with 3 great beaches. Surrounded by an historic medieval wall with narrow streets packed with bars, restaurants and quirky shops.

MUMBLES - GOWER / SWANSEA

A well-loved area of Swansea! One of Dylan Thomas' former stomping grounds and with much to see and do, The Mumbles has something for everyone.

USEFUL INFORMATION

CURRENCY

GBP - Great British Pounds
Debit & Credit Cards - widely accepted.
ATM's - available in most towns and cities.

WALES TRAVEL DISTANCES

Prestatyn to Holyhead - 60 Miles
Holyhead to Bangor - 25 Miles
Bangor to Barmouth - 48 Miles
Barmouth to Aberystwyth - 44 Miles
Aberystwyth to Cardigan - 38 Miles
Cardigan to St Davids - 35 Miles
St Davids to Tenby - 36 Miles
Tenby to The Gower - 60 Miles
The Gower to Cardiff - 60 Miles
Cardiff to Brecon - 42 Miles

EMERGENCY NUMBERS

Police / Ambulance / Fire / Coastguard - 999
AA Roadside Recovery - 0800 88 77 66
RAC Roadside Recovery - 0333 2000 999

HOSPITALS

Wrexham - Maelor Hospital (A & E)
Rhyl - Glan Clwyd Hospital (A & E)
Bangor - Ysbyty Gwynedd (A & E)
Aberystwyth - Bronglais General Hospital (A & E)
Haverfordwest - Withybush General Hospital (A & E)
Carmarthen - Glangwili General Hospital (A & E)
Merthyr Tydfil - Prince Charles Hospital (A & E)
Bridgend - Princess of Wales Hospital (A & E)
Swansea - Morriston Hospital (A & E)
Cardiff - University Hospital of Wales (A & E)
Cwmbran - The Grange University Hospital (A & E)

VETS

Wrexham - Animal Trust Vets CIC - 01978 802658
Llandudno - Vets4Pets - 01492 868970
Aberystwyth - Downes Veterinary Services - 01970 624173
Cardigan - Priory Vets - 01239 612479
Haverfordwest - Fenton Vets - 01437 762806
Swansea - Vets4Pets - 01792 461217
Cardiff - Vets4Pets - 029 2023 2957

CAR REPAIR GARAGES

Bangor - Kwik Fit - 01248 355400
Aberystwyth - Kwik Fit - 01970 625554
Carmarthen - Kwik Fit - 01267 235297
Swansea - Kwik Fit - 01792 651491
Cardiff - Kwik Fit - 029 2034 2837

WELSH PHRASES

"Bore da" – meaning, good morning. Pronounced: 'bore-ray-dah'
"Nos da" – meaning, good night. Pronounced: 'Nohs-dah'
"Sut wyt ti?" – meaning, how are you? Pronounced: 'Soot-wut-tee'
"Diolch" – meaning, thank you. Pronounced: 'Dee-ol-ch'
"Croesco" – meaning, you're welcome. Pronounced: 'Croe-soe'

GENERAL SAFETY

ROADS - Stick to speed limits, be careful when overtaking, in rural areas anticipate livestock, check for motorbikers. Roads can become icy, slippery and flooded - check weather and drive accordingly.

TOWNS & CITIES - Generally safe, hide valuables in vehicle, be aware of pick pockets in busy locations.

MOUNTAINS - Be aware of sheer drops and cliff edges. Dress accordingly, check the weather and avoid climbing in snow and ice.

COASTAL PATHS - Be aware of sheer drops and cliff edges.

BEACHES - Check tide times, some beaches can get cut off. Only swim in safe areas and check information boards. Don't leave valuables unattended on a busy beach.

NORTH WALES & THE BORDERS

NORTH WALES & THE BORDERS

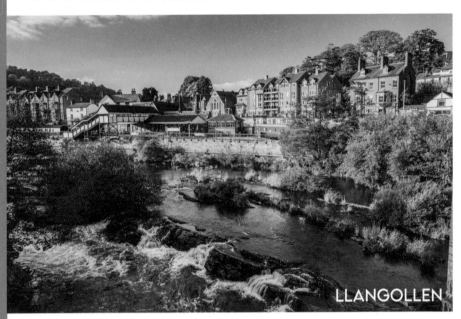

LLANGOLLEN

HISTORIC ARCHITECTURE & NATURAL BEAUTY!

This charming part of Wales has a little something for everyone. From the impressive Pontcysyllte Aqueduct designed by Thomas Telford located within a UNESCO World Heritage Site, to the UK's tallest waterfall - Pistyll Rhaeadr! There is fine mix of rich history and natural beauty to be discovered throughout this region. A warm welcome to Wales.

MUST SEES...

PISTYLL RHAEADR WATERFALL

LLANGOLLEN

PONTCYSYLLTE AQUEDUCT

ERDDIG HALL

THINGS TO SEE AND DO...

PISTYLL RHAEADR WATERFALL

NR LLANRHAEADR, POWYS, SY10 0BZ

///EPIDEMICS.TYPICALLY. SCORES

This 240ft single-drop waterfall is Britain's tallest and will have you amazed at its power and beauty! A short walk from the car park through the gate near the tea room takes you to the base of the falls. If you're feeling a little more adventurous you can view the top of the falls by taking a 20 minute walk up the public footpath. Take care on the paths around the waterfall, they can become slippery when wet. Parking is £5 (there is a small free section just before the main parking site). Opening Times 9:30am - 5:30pm. An absolute must see if you're in the area!

CHIRK CASTLE

LL14 5AF

///CONSOLED.BRAND.BENCH

Magnificent medieval fortress of the Welsh Marches. The castle was built in 1295 by Roger Mortimer de Chirk, uncle of Roger Mortimer, 1st Earl of March as part of King Edward I's chain of fortresses across the north of Wales. It guards the entrance to the Ceiriog Valley. Access to the estate is free, but admission is required to access the castle and gardens. Adults £14.00 / Children £7.00.

PONTCYSYLLTE AQUEDUCT & CANAL WORLD HERITAGE SITE

STATION RD, LLANGOLLEN, LL20 7TY

///BLUNT.CASCADED.PISTON

'Cross the stream in the sky' described by UNESCO as 'a masterpiece of creative genius'. This section of the Llangollen Canal features several embankments, tunnels, viaducts and aqueducts including the staggering Pontcysyllte Aqueduct itself. There are multiple easy to find car parks located nearby and walking across the aqueduct is an experience you'll remember (unless you have a fear of heights like me). As with many locations in Wales, there is a fantastic cafe, tea room, pub & restaurant nearby.

PLAS NEWYDD HISTORIC HOUSE & GARDENS

HILL ST, LLANGOLLEN, LL20 8AW

///SCATTERS.ESCAPES. CRISPS

An interesting historical location with a fascinating story of two women who devoted their lives to converting an unassuming stone cottage into a gothic fantasy. The historic house costs £7.00 for Adults & £6.00 for Children. The gardens and 10 acres of grounds are free to explore if you don't fancy paying the entry fee to check out the house itself.

LLANGOLLEN

LLANGOLLEN, LL20 8PS

///WHISTLE.SMARTING. POLICY

A beautiful town on the River Dee with a wealth of independent shops, cafes, bars & restaurants. Llangollen is part of the UNESCO World Heritage Site along eleven miles of canal from Gledrid to the Horseshoe Falls via the spectacular Pontcysyllte Aqueduct. The postcode and location listed here is the centrally located market street car park.

TOP TIP

YOU CAN TAKE A BOAT TRIP ACROSS THE 'STREAM IN THE SKY' – THE PONTCYSYLLTE AQUEDUCT!

PONTCYSYLLTE AQUEDUCT

HORSESHOE FALLS
LLANGOLLEN,
LL20 8BN
///REFORMING.TRADES.
ABLE

Another piece of Thomas Telford engineering! This weir was designed to draw water from the River Dee in to the canal and at 140m long is a sight to behold. You can enjoy a scenic walk from the town passing by the impressive chain bridge on your way to Horseshoe falls.

CASTELL DINAS BRAN
LLANGOLLEN,
LL20 8D
///UNDERWAY.PRAWN.
SUPPOSING

The rugged remains of a medieval castle towering high above the surrounding Dee Valley. The castle was built in the 1260's by one of the princes of Powys. Parking is available on the roadside and a 20-minute walk will bring you to the top of the hill! The views on top are sublime!

TY NANT OUTDOORS
LLANGOLLEN,
LL20 8EG
///FABRICATE.
DANGEROUSLY.AIRSTRIP

Ty Nant is a highly recommended outdoor adventure company offering a range of adrenaline fueled and calmer pursuits including kayaking across the Pontcysyllte Aqueduct & whitewater kayaking. If you want to add a unique activity into your road trip itinerary, Ty Nant is the place to go in this part of Wales.

ERDDIG HALL
ERDDIG,
WREXHAM,
LL13 0YT
///BANGLE.SEVERE.RACE

A monumental Grade-1 National Trust property in Wrexham with the second largest collection of items (30,000) in the whole of the National Trust. The vast gardens, exuberant servants rooms and scenic parkland present Erddig as enjoyable afternoon or morning out. Dogs are allowed in most of the estate (apart from the building itself). Tickets for the whole property are £14.00 for Adults and £7.00 for Children.

WREXHAM
WREXHAM,
LL13 8AE
///AWAKE.ADJUST.JUMPY

Wrexham has traded in its historical market town title for its recently awarded city status. The city has a mix of *'artistic culture to historic treasures, buzzing nightlife to splendid countryside.'* Ty Pawb is a vibrant community space and the cultural heart of the city built from a former indoor market. You may have been aware of the recent developments at Wrexham AFC which has been acquired by famous actors Ryan Reynolds and Rob McElhenny. They've become ambassadors for the city and helped welcome new fans and international visitors. Wrexham is a solid base to explore the aforementioned Erdigg Hall, UNESCO World Heritage viaducts and Llangollen. Did you know that the very first Miss World came from here?

@ROBBIEROAMS

PISTYLL RHAEADR WATERFALL

WHERE TO STAY...

CAMPING, MOTORHOMES AND CARAVANS

WERN ISAF FARM
WERN RD, LLANGOLLEN, LL20 8DU | 01978 860632

Wern Isaf is principally a working farm, situated half a mile from the centre of bustling little Llangollen, at just sufficient elevation to give the gently sloping camping field an unobstructed view out over the lovely Dee Valley. What may not be apparent from up here is the fact that almost everything you could possibly want to do from a campsite can be done from here.

FACILITIES...
ELECTRIC HOOKUP
TOILETS
SHOWERS
DOG FRIENDLY
WASTE DISPOSAL

LLYN RHYS CAMPSITE
WREXHAM, LL11 3AF | 01978 790627

Llyn Rhys Campite is the ideal base for mountain bikers and walkers being 5 minutes from the Coed Llandegla Forest Mountain Bike Centre and the Offa's Dyke Path. Based in an Area of Outstanding Natural Beauty.

FACILITIES...
ELECTRIC HOOKUP
TOILETS
SHOWERS
DOG FRIENDLY
WASTE DISPOSAL

HOTELS, BNB'S AND ACCOMMODATION

GALES WINE BAR | ££-£££
18 BRIDGE ST, LLANGOLLEN, LL20 8PF | 01978 860089

Situated in one of the oldest streets in Llangollen and a few seconds from the high street, Gales has 15 en-suite bedrooms. High rating on Trip Advisor & Booking.com

LLANGOLLEN SHEPHERDS HUTS | £££
GERAINT, LLANGOLLEN, LL20 8AA | 07812 350712

The luxury and traditional handmade shepherd huts exude vintage and rustic ambiance. A nice quirky option with a little bit of charm and luxury mixed together.

THE LEMON TREE | ££-£££
29 RHOSDDU RD, WREXHAM, LL11 2LP | 01978 261211

In Wrexham town centre, the Lemon Tree Hotel offers stylish rooms with character features. With free WiFi and free parking, there is also a restaurant. Great location.

TOP TIP

TRY THE PONTCYSYLLTE CHAPEL TEA ROOM IF YOU STOP AT THE AQUEDUCT!

CASTELL DINAS BRAN

WHERE TO EAT & DRINK 🍽️

S&G BISTRO | BREAKFAST & FABULOUS PIZZAS
17 CASTLE STREET, LLANGOLLEN, LL20 8NY

RIVERBANC | BREAKFAST, BRUNCH & CAFE
BRIDGE STREET, LLANGOLLEN, LL20 8PF

THE BANK WINE BAR AND BISTRO | TAPAS & SMALL PLATES
43 HIGH STREET, WREXHAM, LL13 8HY

THE HIDEOUT BISTRO & BAR | GREAT ALL ROUNDER & SUNDAY ROASTS
MACHINE HOUSE CHESTER ROAD, WREXHAM, LL12 0HW

A WONDERFUL WELSH WEEKEND!

We recently visited this region for a weekend away with our friends Laura & Ryan. It was Laura's Birthday so we decided to stay in a small cottage (booked on Airbnb) located around 25 minutes from the iconic Pistyll Rhaeadr waterfall. The cottage was situated just outside a tiny village that contained little more than a few houses but importantly, had a cracking country pub which we made use of! Although the weather was pants for the entire weekend, the surrounding valleys and countryside were wonderful and being able to switch off from our everyday lives in these lovely surroundings did everyone the world of good. On the Saturday, we visited the aforementioned Pistyll Rhaeadr waterfall. This was my first visit here and I have to say, what an amazing spectacle it is! As the UK's tallest single drop waterfall, my expectations were high. Having seen waterfalls all over Scotland and many across the world, I didn't think I'd be so impressed with this place. The sheer power and beauty of Pistyll Rhaedar is something to behold. It was a wet and miserable old day, but this waterfall picked us all right up. Other than the tight single track road leading to the waterfall, getting here is straightforward. We parked in the free area (just before the main car park) and walked a few minutes to the base where you can take some wonderful photos!

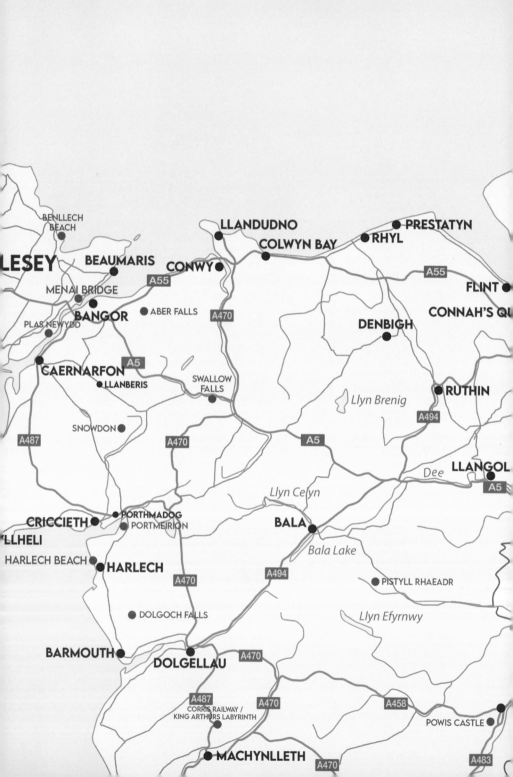

THE
NORTH
COAST

THE NORTH COAST

CONWY CASTLE

A FUN SEEKERS PARADISE!

Sitting on the northern coastline, this area has several considerable seaside towns which are crammed full of history, beaches and a lot of fun things to do! From the must see UNESCO world heritage site of Conwy to the light-hearted towns of Rhyl & Prestatyn, you are guaranteed a good time and some fabulous fresh fish and chips!

MUST SEES...
CONWY & CONWY CASTLE
LLANDUDNO
COLWYN BAY
PENRHYN CASTLE & GARDEN

THINGS TO SEE AND DO...

RHYL & PRESTATYN

RHYL LL18 1HD
///YARN.TINS.EXISTS

PRESTATYN LL19 9AA
///POLICE.LIVING.REGRESS

Missed out by many guidebooks and often scoffed at, Rhyl and the nearby town of Prestatyn have a wealth of things to do and see. If you don't take yourself too seriously you can have some great fun exploring the several beaches in the area. The Rhyl miniature railway and the Gronant Dunes – a site of special scientific interest home to rare species such as the sand lizard and natterjack toad. Like many sea side towns across Wales, the fish and chips in Rhyl & Prestatyn are top notch.

 @ROBBIEROAMS

COLWYN BAY
LL29 8DF
///WARNS.DEBATE.INCOMES

A seaside town in North Wales famous for Colwyn Bay Beach – a notably clean and sandy dog friendly beach located near to the town which has several shops and restaurants. The Welsh Mountain Zoo is also located withing the town and has a solid overall 4.4 star rating on Google – perfect for a couple of hours of exploring.

LLANDUDNO
LL30 1AN
///RECLINE.UNSTATED.
IMPOSE

The starting point for our recent Wales 400 mile road trip (watch the full video on my YouTube channel to get more tips and tricks). Llandudno is the quintessential Welsh Victorian seaside town. Like Rhyl, it may not appeal to all, but look a little closer and you'll find it really packs a punch! It has a great pier, a unique cable car offering fantastic views of the surrounding area and of course fantastic fish and chip shops! The coastal town was named 'fish and chip capital' for the whole of Wales in 2022. If you want some light hearted fun and a potential start / end point for your road trip, look no further. Just be mindful of the seagulls! They are built differently in North Wales and will make light work of a fresh ice cream or cone of chips. Cling on to that cone of chips like your life depended on it!

CONWY & CONWY CASTLE
LL32 8AY
///RECRUITER.RESPONSES.
ETCHINGS

A world heritage site home to the imposing thirteenth-century 'Conwy Castle'. Conwy has a little bit of something for everyone and I would recommend at least a short walk around its historic centre which is filled with great eateries, pubs and shops. Its medieval Castle, which still towers over the town after 700 years, is of course the main selling point and can be explored with entry for £11.10 for adults and £7.80 for children. Within Conway is also the *'Smallest House in Britain'* measuring just 72 inches across and 122 inches high. If all of the historical information and facts become too much for you, why not escape to Bodnant Garden, one of Wales' best gardens – perfect to relax and unwind. 'Conwy' is actually pronounced 'Con-Wee' and not 'Con-Way' much to the disbelief of many visitors. All in all, a fantastic town with world heritage status and it's 100% a must see if your road trip happens to pass through the North Coast of Wales.

CONWY CASTLE & TOWN

BANGOR
LL57 1LA
///RESCUER.HAPPEN.
ECOLOGIST

This cathedral city is in fact the oldest city in Wales (I bet you didn't know that did you?). Bangor is a solid base from which to explore Snowdonia or even the nearby Anglesey from. It has the main shops and supermarkets should you need to stock up on any supplies before heading into Snowdonia. As Bangor is also a University city, there is a host of pubs, clubs and great places to eat. Check out Domu, a family run, independent coffee house offering some unique Eastern Europe food served fresh every day. Bangor is also home to Garth Pier, the second longest Pier in Wales which offers superb views over to Anglesey and is worth checking out if you're in town.

PENRHYN CASTLE AND GARDEN
BANGOR
LL57 4HT
///VILLAS.HIRED.STRICTEST

Bangor is also the location of the mighty Penrhyn Castle – a neo-Norman build 'crammed' with fascinating items such as a one-ton slate bed made for Queen Victoria. The unique architecture, opulent interiors and fine art collection sit alongside a history of sugar and slate fortunes, of social unrest and the longest-running industrial dispute in British history. Little explorers can climb trees, make dens and run wild in the adventure playground. Adult tickets are £13.00 and Childrens tickets are £6.50. You are certainly spoilt for choice with castles in North Wales!

PENRHYN CASTLE – BANGOR

LLANDUDNO PIER

WHERE TO STAY...

CAMPING, MOTORHOMES AND CARAVANS

DINARTH HALL FARM
DINERTH HALL RD, LLANDUDNO, LL28 4PX | 01492 548203

Within easy reach of Anglesey and Snowdonia, Dinarth Hall Camping is a friendly, family-run site, structured around a working farm. There's a huge supply of electric hook up pitches, hot showers and all the usual facilities. The site opens at Easter and closes during the winter so it's best to book before arriving.

FACILITIES...
ELECTRIC HOOKUP
TOILETS
SHOWERS
DOG FRIENDLY
WASTE DISPOSAL

DINAS FARM SITE
BANGOR, LL57 4NB | 01248 364227

Family run campsite near to Bangor offering a very warm welcome. Recently refurbished toilet and shower block. Dogs are welcome. As campsites go, there aren't many more relaxing than this with the sound of the river in the background.

FACILITIES...
ELECTRIC HOOKUP
TOILETS
SHOWERS
DOG FRIENDLY
WASTE DISPOSAL

HOTELS, BNB'S AND ACCOMMODATION

ST. GEORGE'S HOTEL | £££
ST GEORGE'S PL, LLANDUDNO LL30 2LG | 01492 877544

Originally opened in 1854, today the St George's hotel offers excellent service, incredible sea views, and surroundings so comfortable you won't want to leave!

TAN Y BRYN GLAMPING | £££
BRYNPYDEW RD, LLANDUDNO JUNCTION LL31 9JZA | 01492 549296

Fancy a unique slice of luxury in Llandudno? These luxury glamping pods come with a private hot tub, all individually designed offering a unique glamping stay. Lovely stuff.

THE SLATE | ££-£££
TAL Y BONT, BANGOR, LL57 3UR | 01248 355500

A highly recommended hotel set in a converted 1700s farmhouse which has received a recent rennovation. There's also a fantastic food & drink offering!

TOP TIP

IF YOU HEAD TO LLANDUDNO - MAKE SURE TO GO ON THE CABLE CAR!

RHYL BEACH

WHERE TO EAT & DRINK 🍽️

THE LOAF COFFEE & SANDWICH BAR | BREAKFAST & LUNCH
12-14 GLODDAETH STREET, LLANDUDNO, LL30 2DS

BARNACLES FISH & CHIPS | FISH & CHIPS
7 MOSTYN ST, LLANDUDNO, LL30 2NL

DOMU | COFFEE & HEARTY EAST EUROPEAN FOOD
206 HIGH STREET, BANGOR, LL57 1NY

BANGOR TANDOORI RESTAURANT | INDIAN & BALTI
360 HIGH STREET, BANGOR, LL57 1YE

A DOGS DAY OUT AT THE FAIR!

We started our recent Welsh Coast 400 Road Trip at the picturesque town of Llandudno in North Wales. After managing to bag a decent parking spot next to the promenade we took a pleasant walk to end of the pier. From here we took in some great views out to sea, soaked up the atmosphere and watched the terrydactyl sized seagulls reaping havoc for anyone in possession of a cone of chips. The sun was shining, we were in good spirits and this Welsh seaside town felt like a perfect place to start our epic road trip! On the pier we noticed a sign next to the ferris wheel saying 'dogs allowed' and so we duly obliged and took Archie and Gem for their first ever fairground ride. Don't get me wrong, to some dogs this would have been terrifying and quite a cruel thing to put them through. Fortunately we know our dogs very well and although Archie was a little unsure to start with, after a couple of minutes he was thoroughly enjoying himself. Gem was unphased throughout. The views were fantastic and a good time was had by all. Wales is very accommodating for dogs and why should they be left out eh? (The nearby cable car also allows dogs if you are looking for dog friendly options in Llandudno). We ended our stop in Llandudno with an ice cream which was nearly nabbed by one of them pesky seagulls! Please be careful, they will swoop and take any food you have on you without hesitation!

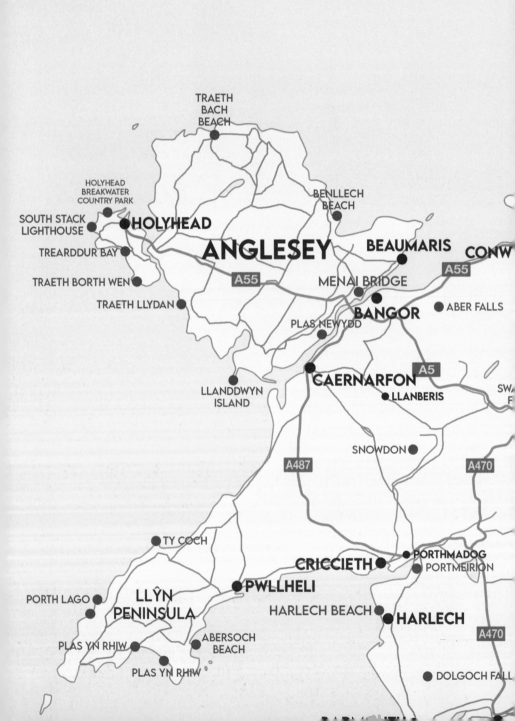

ANGLESEY

MENAI SUSPENSION BRIDGE

ANGLESEY

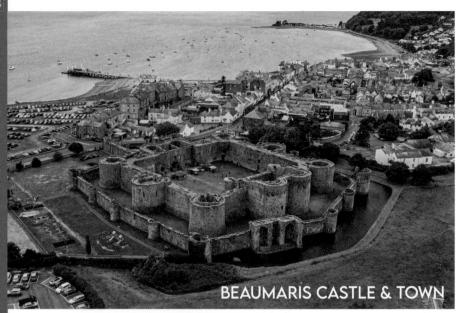

BEAUMARIS CASTLE & TOWN

THE WELSH ISLAND THAT HAS IT ALL!

I think of Anglesey as a mini-island version of Wales. It really does have everything! From ancient castles to picture perfect lighthouses, blue flag beaches to wild forests. You'll be amazed by how much there is to actually experience on this small but mighty island. It makes for a perfect weekend destination if you're short on time...

MUST SEES...

MENAI SUSPENSION BRIDGE

BEAUMARIS CASTLE

SOUTH STACK LIGHTHOUSE

LLANDDWYN ISLAND

THINGS TO SEE AND DO...

MENAI SUSPENSION BRIDGE

LL59 5EA
///COMICAL.OTHERWISE.DOCTOR

An Anglesey landmark! So, you may be thinking it's a little unusual for a bridge to be on the must-see list, but this thing is a piece of engineering beauty! Designed by Thomas Telford and completed in 1826, the Menai Suspension Bridge was the world's first major suspension bridge. It's incredible that after almost 200 years of operation, this Grade 1 listed structure still carries road traffic from the mainland over to the island of Anglesey. On the mainland side of the bridge there's a small road where you can park to get some photos and even walk across the bridge to get some views across the Menai Strait.

BEAUMARIS
LL58 8AL
///TRACE.BOILS.EXPAND

A historic seaside town filled with a mix of medieval, Georgian, Victorian and Edwardian architecture. You absolutely must take a walk through the town with its charming streets and picturesque cottages. There are a number of popular cafes, pubs, restaurants and shops. You'll also be able to see the oldest house in Wales which was built in around 1400. A charming little town that we really enjoyed and I think you will too!

BEAUMARIS CASTLE
LL58 8AL
///QUESTIONS.CABIN.JUMPY

The final piece of the puzzle for Edward I after already constructing the mighty castles of Conwy, Caernarfon and Harlech. Beaumaris is famous for being the *greatest castle never built*. This was intended to be the crowning glory, but a lack of money and trouble in Scotland meant that building work petered out by the 1320's and the project was never properly finished. Don't be put off by the story, Beaumaris is a fortress of immense size and 'near-perfect symmetry'. Visiting this World Heritage Site is a must do for history enthusiasts and a great stop off for children. Adult tickets are £8.30 and Children £5.80. Dogs on leads are welcome to access ground floor levels of the castle. The seaside town of Beaumaris is also a fantastic location that is worth an hour of exploration.

BEAUMARIS GAOL & COURTHOUSE
STEEPLE LN,
LL58 8EP
///JOGGING.RELATIVES.BACKSWING

Explore the dimly lit corridors and places of punishment at the famous Beaumaris Gaol and Courthouse. The walls of this Victorian prison hold many secrets which you can discover upon your visit. Combined entry to both venues is £9.50 for Adults & £7.50 for Children.

BENLLECH BEACH
BAY VIEW RD,
BENLLECH,
LL74 8TT
///FEWEST.CAMPFIRES.PRODUCT

This has to be one of the best beaches on the island! Benllech has fine golden sand and clear blue waters which are very safe for bathing if you're brave enough to face the brisk Welsh sea (or maybe you can just watch everyone else giving it a go). There are excellent facilities and easy access for wheelchairs and prams. Although the weather wasn't great when I last visited, I could really imagine this place in the sunshine with kites being flown, people bodyboarding and picnics being devoured. If you forgot your beach picnic, the local chippy (Finney's) is highly rated!

SOUTH STACK LIGHTHOUSE

CEMAES BAY TRAETH BACH BEACH
FFORDD Y TRAETH,
CEMAES BAY,
LL67 0ET
///GUILTY.BATH.MOUTHS

Another quaint seaside location offering a great beach, decent parking, a choice of pubs and even a beach side wood fired pizza shack! The harbour makes for a fantastic photo and when the tide is out we noticed a vast selection of rockpools to explore if that's your thing. Camaes has shallow water making it ideal for kids and apparently the local butcher shop offers a unique pork and seaweed sausage! Why the hell not?

HOLYHEAD BREAKWATER COUNTRY PARK
HOLYHEAD,
LL65 1YG
///GRACED.MUFFIN.
REPLAYED

Located near the town of Holyhead, the breakwater country park was opened in 1990 and is set on the site of an old quarry. The park offers a mix of wildlife, history and breathtaking scenery with many walks and trails available. If you're lucky you may be able to spot peregrine falcons, grey seals and the illusive 'StenaLine' ferry leaving for Ireland! What a scenic part of Wales!

SOUTH STACK LIGHTHOUSE
HOLYHEAD,
LL65 2UL
///UNREALISTIC.RATES.
SKYLIGHTS

Perched on its own tiny island of the west coast, South Stack is a jaw dropping location that simply must be on any Anglesey itinerary. The lighthouse can be viewed from the adjacent cliff tops for free or for a close up, can be reached via 400 steps and a bridge located high above the powerful waves below (ticket required for tours of the lighthouse). For keen bird watchers or wildlife enthusiasts, South Stack is a perfect place to watch 1000's of breeding seabirds including guillemots, razorbills and puffins. South Stack also has a RSPB Café.

TREARDDUR BAY
HOLYHEAD,
LL65 2UP
///TABLETS.PACES.
CONFIGURE

A charming beach sloping gently into the sea with rockpools and slipways. This dog friendly location offers a perfect setting to watch the sunset or have a lazy morning (weather dependent). With good parking, public toilets and several places to eat or drink, you have everything you need nearby. I was really impressed with how clean the beach was and how friendly the locals were.

PORTH DIANA BEACH & PORTH CASTELL BEACH
LL65 2AQ
///TABLETS.PACES.
CONFIGURE

Located less than a mile from Treardurr Bay, Porth Diana and Porth Castell are two relatively small but beautiful beaches that offer more of that Treardurr charm! With crystal clear waters and rocky outcrops, both of these coves are ideal for paddle boarding and bathing. If you're feeling brave, there are a few suitable rocks for jumping off into deeper water.

LLANDDWYN ISLAND

BWA DU / BWA GWYN
RHOSCOLYN,
LL65 2SQ
///NOUN.NEXT.GOAT
///NEATER.CALLERS.
REVERTED

These two unique sea stacks located on the Anglesey Coastal Path near to Rhoscolyn, reward those who are daring enough to cross the headland to view them. Please take care if you do walk along the cliff side to these sea stacks as the cliff edges are dangerous and have sheer drops.

TRAETH BORTH WEN
RHOSCOLYN,
LL65 2NX
///SNUG.NECKLACES.AIMED

Another beautiful beach on Holyhead that's relatively quiet compared to others in the area. The water is calm making it perfect for paddle boarding, kayaking or swimming. There's a small beach car park and this is also a really popular location for dog walkers.

TRAETH LLYDAN
HOLYHEAD,
LL65 2RZ
///PLAUSIBLE.RECEPTION.
INFLATING

Llydan is a hidden gem of a beach which is situated in the Anglesey Area of Outstanding Natural Beauty. Located just 2.5 miles from the previously mentioned 'Borth Wen' beach on Holyhead Island, this place reminds me of several of the wild and wonderful beaches in the Scottish Highlands. Just a heads up, you may be disturbed every now and then by the local RAF base (unless of course you enjoy plane spotting).

TRAETH CRIGYLL
HOLYHEAD,
LL65 3NY
///BRIEFER.MOVES.
UPPERMOST

An ideal location to watch the planes departing from the nearby RAF Valley. This wide sandy beach (less than a mile from the centre of Rhosneigr) is backed by idyllic dunes and is a top spot for windsurfing and kite boarding.

NEWBOROUGH FOREST / LLANDDWYN ISLAND
LLANFAIRPWLLGWYN-
GYLL, LL61 6SG
///SMOKING.SNOOZING.
WHIZZED

A photographer's dream! Llanddwyn is a small tidal island on the west coast of Angelsey is home to the ruins of St. Dwynwen church and two very scenic lighthouses - Twr Bach and Twr Mawr. Park at the Newborough Forest car park and make the 4 mile return walk either through the lush forest or along the beach to Llanddwyn Island. Try and avoid high tide when the island is cut off from the mainland and remember that this place is very exposed to the elements. I faced a barrage of torrential rain and very strong winds when visiting here, however, it meant I had the entire island to myself (a part from a few wild horses). Even in bad weather this place was a joy to experience and was certainly worth the walk from the car park. One of the most picturesque locations in the whole of Wales – on my watch, this is a must see!

@ROBBIEROAMS

ANGLESEY SEA ZOO
LLANFAIRPWLL,
LL61 6TQ
///NOTED.OVEN.LATER

A unique aquarium with over 40 tanks displaying the best of British marine wildlife! Located on the South East of Anglesey, the Sea Zoo is a potential rainy day escape and is only 20 odd minutes from Newborough Forest & Llandwyn Island.

PLAS NEWYDD HOUSE AND GARDENS
LLANFAIRPWLLGWYN-
GYLL,
LL61 6DQ
///RISEN.CRACKS.CRINKLED

Described by the National Trust as an *'enchanting mansion and gardens, with spectacular views of Snowdonia'*. Set on the shores of the Menai Strait, this country house offers a unique Anglesey destination for those with an interest in history, nature and art. After exploring the house & grounds there is an onsite café to indulge in. Tickets are £11.00 for Adults and £5.50 for Children (unless you own a National Trust membership). Dogs are permitted in certain areas of the grounds, but the £11.00 entry is probably not worth it if you do bring your four legged friend.

RIBRIDE
PORTH DANIEL,
WATER ST, MENAI
BRIDGE, LL59 5DE
///OUTNUMBER.NOTICING.
OTTER

A unique and action-packed way to experience some of the marvelous sights along the Menai Straight. RibRide offer numerous adrenaline-fueled boat trips from March to November and to give you an idea on prices, their 'Bridges and Swellies' tour is £30 per person for a 60 minute adventure.

ISLE OF ANGLESEY COASTAL PATH
HOLYHEAD,
LL65 1WY
///GOLF.REMOVER.RELISHED

A huge attraction for walkers! This 130 mile route offers the very best sights in Anglesey and also caters for cyclists and horse riders in certain sections. Walkers will experience a mix of farmland, coastal heath, dunes, salt-marsh, cliffs and small pockets of woodland. The route starts at St Cybi's Church in Holyhead. Now I doubt that many of you will be looking to walk 130 miles whilst on a road trip, however, the section from Trearddur Bay to Holyhead is around 12 miles and will take 5 hours. During this route you'll pass many of Anglesey's main attractions including South Stack Lighthouse, Holyhead Mountain, North Stack, Breakwater Country Park and St Cybi's Church. This could be a fantastic way to spend a morning or afternoon if your legs and feet allow it!

TOP TIP

100% DO THE 4 MILE RETURN WALK TO LLANDWYN ISLAND, IT'S STUNNING!

WHERE TO STAY...

CAMPING, MOTORHOMES AND CARAVANS

PEN Y BONT TOURING & CAMPSITE

FOUR MILE BRIDGE, VALLEY, LL65 3EY | 01407 740481

A warm and friendly welcome awaits you at Pen y Bont – a small, family run touring caravan and camping site which has been run by the same family for over 50 years. Centrally located, this campsite is a perfect base for exploring the attractions on Holyhead. Situated in an area of outstanding natural beauty, you can spot a variety of birds, swans, geese, fauna and wildflowers all from the campsite.

FACILITIES...
ELECTRIC HOOKUP
TOILETS
SHOWERS
DOG FRIENDLY
WASTE DISPOSAL

AWELFRYN CAMPSITE

LLANFAIRPWLLGWYNGYLL, LL61 6SG | 07906 017489

Situated approximately one mile from Llanddwyn beach in an area of outstanding natural beauty with fantastic views overlooking the mountains of Snowdonia and the Llyn Peninsula. Access to Llanddwyn Island via a short walk along the beach.

FACILITIES...
ELECTRIC HOOKUP
TOILETS
SHOWERS
DOG FRIENDLY
WASTE DISPOSAL

HOTELS, BNB'S AND ACCOMMODATION

TREARDDUR BAY HOTEL | ££-£££

LON ISALLT, TREARDDUR BAY, LL65 2UN | 01407 860301

Fabulous sea views and balconies and all with the comforts you'll need for a relaxing break. Located right by the beach, ideal for seaside views while you cosy up in the onsite pub.

BISHOPSGATE HOUSE HOTEL & RESTAURANT | £££

54 CASTLE ST, BEAUMARIS, LL58 8BB | 01248 810302

Modern amenities have been blended with antique beds and carefully chosen decor, to ensure that your stay is as comfortable as possible. Ideal location within Beaumaris!

PODS PWLL COCH - GLAMPING PODS | ££-£££

PWLL COCH ISAF, AMLWCH, LL68 9RA | 07769 708725

Luxury glamping pods completely self-contained with the option of your own hot tub! If you're looking for something a little bit different, why not stay here?

TOP TIP

THE SEA SHANTY CAFE IS A FAVOURITE FOR BOTH LOCALS AND TOURISTS!

TREARDURR BAY

WHERE TO EAT & DRINK 🍽

CATCH 22 BRASSERIE | BRITISH & INTERNATIONAL DISHES
LONDON ROAD, VALLEY, LL65 3DP

SEA SHANTY CAFE | SEAFOOD & BRITISH
TREARDDUR BAY, HOLYHEAD LL65 2YR

HAPPY VALLEY PAVILION | DELICIOUS CAKES & COFFEE
GREEN EDGE BOWLING GREEN, BEAUMARIS, LL58 8BY

HARRY'S BISTRO | TRADITIONAL AND CONTEMPORARY FOOD
HENLLYS, HENLLYS LN, LLAN-FAES, BEAUMARIS LL58 8HU

WE COULDN'T SEE A THING!

A few years ago, me and Jas went on a weekend trip to Anglesey. Not really knowing much about the island we made a rough plan to stop at South Stack Lighthouse & Llanddwyn Island as our main priorities. We stayed in a hotel in Holyhead after arriving on the Friday evening. The following morning we were up bright and early and headed straight to South Stack Lighthouse where I was hoping to take some wonderful photos of the sunrise. Unfortunately, mother nature had other plans as when we arrived, there was a thick blanket of fog making visibility around 4 metres at best. Not only could I not get a photo of South Stack Lighthouse, I couldn't even bloody see it! The same was true of Llandwyn Island as the fog engulfed Anglesey. We drove home gutted about the weekend slightly being ruined by the fog. Anyway, a few years later and we returned to South Stack. This time the weather was much improved and I finally got my photo (see page 79). South Stack Lighthouse is remarkable place that I'm so glad I returned to and even better now I get to share my photos and experiences with you. PS. I also returned to Llanddwyn where the fog was replaced with 60mph gales and torrential rain. This wasn't all bad as me and Archie had the island to ourselves!

LLŶN PENINSULA

LLŶN PENINSULA

PORTHDINLLAEN LIFEBOAT STATION

THE SECRECT CORNER OF WALES!

The Llyn peninsula is a destination that I'm sure most of us wouldn't be able to point to on a map. It's a relatively unknown corner of Wales that is overlooked by nearby Snowdonia and Anglesey, however, this Area of Outstanding Natural Beauty offers some of the best scenery in the whole of Wales. You won't be disappointed...

MUST SEES...

NEFYN BEACH

TY COCH INN

WHISTLING
SANDS BEACH

HELLS MOUTH BEACH

CRICCIETH CASTLE

THINGS TO SEE AND DO...

LLŶN COASTAL PATH

ABERDARON,
PWLLHELI,
LL53 8LH
///EVOKED.VALIDATED.
MEMORY

If you're a keen walker, the Llyn peninsula is a must visit! Jump onto the Llyn coastal path (part of the national coastal path) and take in some of the amazing views & breath-taking wildlife. The path from Porth Oer to Aberdaron is around 14km and will take around 4 hours. There are numerous routes you can follow depending on your time restraints. A hidden gem located on the coastal walk near Trefor is the Trefor Sea Stacks which can be found by following the coastal path West from Trefor beach. This place offers some wonderful photo opportunities.

NEFYN BEACH
LL53 6ED
///TIES.INCISIONS.SAME

The small village of Nefyn, on the isolated north coast of the Llyn Peninsula, has a long, sandy bay, sheltered by the beautiful Nefyn Headland, and backed by steep slopes. Nefyn Beach itself is something of a hidden gem, known for its clear blue waters along with stunning views of the bay. Please take care when walking down to the beach, since many paths are quite steep.

TY COCH INN
PORTHDINLLAEN,
MORFA NEFYN,
PWLLHELI,
LL53 6DB
///MASSIVE.DANCE.BRINK

A pub literally located on a beach in the village of Porthdinllaen that was once voted *as one of the top 10 beach bars in the whole world*. The crazy thing about Ty Coch is that you can't reach the pub by car and can only do so by walking or by boat. To get here park at the Lon Golff national trust car park (or the golf club car park) and walk across the golf course for around 20 minutes. Alternatively, you can follow 'Beach Road' but access is restricted at high tide. The pub serves delicious food and there can't be many better places to enjoy a pint!

PORTH IAGO
RHOSHIRWAUN,
GWYNEDD,
LL53 8LP
///AGENCY.BALLOONED.
RECEIVING

One of the most picturesque beaches on the Llyn peninsula! If the weather and lighting is right, this beach really wouldn't be out of place in the Caribbean! It's somewhat of a hidden gem and it even made it onto The Guardians *'Top 10 Secret Beaches in Wales List'* a few years ago. The white sand & turquoise waters are even dog friendly and there's a fantastic campsite (based on a farm) right above the beach.

TRAETH PORTHOR / WHISTLING SANDS BEACH
ABERDARON,
PWLLHELI,
LL53 8LH
///EVOKED.VALIDATED.
MEMORY

Arguably the best beach on the Llyn peninsula! Traeth Porthor has beautiful golden sands which slopes gradually into the sea making it ideal for bathing (although there may not be a lifeguard on duty so take care). This beach really reminds of some of the fabulous Scottish Highland beaches such as Strathy Bay or Sango Sands. Accessing the beach is possible from the National Trust car park down a relatively steep hill so take everything you need for the beach to avoid an annoying trip back to the car park! It will be busier here in the summer months and unfortunately dogs aren't allowed from April-September, however, the beach is located on coastal path so there are plenty of walking and photo opportunities here.

PORTH IAGO

ABERDARON BEACH
ABERDARON,
PWLLHELI,
LL53 8BE
///INFLATION.BAKER.
GROCERS

Another beautiful beach? Surely you can't be bored of them yet? Aberdaron is a mile long sandy beach which has plenty to explore including sea caves and rock pools, the coast path leads to small beaches in both directions. Windsurfing, kayaking and sailing are popular activities as are boat trips, including summertime trips to Bardsey Island from nearby Porth Meudwy.

PLAS YN RHIW
PLAS YN RHIW,
PWLLHELI,
LL53 8AB
///PLANKTON.ROOST.
BROWNISH

A charming manor house with 'ornamental garden' operated by the National Trust. Although dogs aren't allowed everywhere at Plas Yn Rhiw, you can still walk them around certain parts of the grounds and take them to the onsite tea room.

PORTH NEIGWL / HELLS MOUTH
LLANENGAN,
ABERSOCH,
LL53 7LG
///EXIT.PHEASANTS.FADE

A 3-mile-wide beach offering dramatic views and powerful waves ideal for surfers or bodyboarders. Porth Neigwl known as 'Hells Mouth' in English is rarely busy making it perfect for a peaceful walk (dogs are allowed). There are no facilities here so potentially bring a picnic and make the short walk along the dunes from the car park to experience this wild and wonderful location.

ABERSOCH BEACH
ABERSOCH,
GWYNEDD,
LL53 7DP
///MANGO.ADMIRES.BEND

Originally a fishing port, now a popular seaside resort, Abersoch has a large, relatively sheltered sandy beach on the southeast facing side of the Llyn Peninsula. Abersoch (a blue flag beach) is considered to be safe for swimmers and the town hosts an annual summer jazz & music festival that might take your fancy. The beach huts make for a compelling photo that I'm sure will end up on your Facebook or Instagram.

PWLLHELI MARIAN-Y-DE BEACH
CARDIGAN COURT,
PWLLHELI,
LL53 5PG
///PUFFED.DUPE.VERGE

North Wales has a remarkable number of wonderful beaches and the Llyn Peninsula is no different. Pwllheli beach is a long quiet beach with dog friendly sections and an easily accessible car park over the road. Pwllheli is particularly good to stretch the legs and take in some of that fresh sea air. The town has a number of shops, eateries and a marina. A difficult name to pronounce in Welsh or English! A safe bet would be to call it 'Puh-theh-lee' and most locals will understand this no problem.

@ROBBIEROAMS

BEACH HUTS AT ABERSOCH BEACH

CRICCIETH CASTLE

GLASFRYN PARC
Y FFÔR,
PWLLHELI,
LL53 6PG
///ADMITS.SECURE.
ANCHORMAN

The ultimate place for a fun day out! With 13 different activities including go karting, ten pin bowling, clay pigeon shooting, archery, inflatable aqua park and more, Glasfryn Parc is a fabulous destination to mix up your road trip. It's located in the centre of the Llyn Peninsula between Pwllheli and Llanaelhaearn. So if you've had enough of the beautiful beaches on the peninsula, give this place a go!

CRICCIETH CASTLE
CASTLE ST,
CRICCIETH,
LL52 0DP
///MODERATED.OFFERS.
AWAITED

Criccieth Castle is a native Welsh castle sitting majestically above Tremadog bay. Supposedly built in the 13th century, the remains now make for an interesting visit (tickets required – Adults £6.50 / Children - £4.60). There are fantastic coastline views from within the castle and if you don't fancy paying the admission fee, visit the nearby Criccieth beach to get a lovely postcard style photo of the castle! Always check opening times online before visiting.

CRICCIETH BEACH
CRICCIETH,
GWYNEDD,
LL52 0HU
///CORKSCREW.CONSPIRE.
SIDEBURNS

A mixture of sand and shingle with a picturesque view towards the imposing 13th century 'Criccieth Castle'. This beach can be accessed from many points along the promenade and has a dog friendly area to the east section. The small town of Criccieth has a range of shops, cafes and pubs that may well be calling your name when you make your visit.

TOP TIP

WANT AN EPIC PHOTO OF CRICCIETH CASTLE SIMILAR TO THE ONE ON THE LEFT? HEAD TO CRICCIETH BEACH DURING SUNSET OR SUNRISE AND TAKE YOUR PHOTO STOOD ON THE SECTION BEHIND CADWALDERS ICE CREAM SHOP. WHAT3WORDS LOCATION BELOW...
///REAP.ENCROACH.STREAKS

WHERE TO STAY...

CAMPING, MOTORHOMES AND CARAVANS

TREHELI FARM CAMPSITE
RHIW, PWLLHELI, LL53 8AA | 07805 594337

Treheli Farm is a stunning Caravan & Campsite in a rustic hideaway, situated in the corner of Hell's Mouth bay. The site offers unparalleled views over Cardigan Bay. The beautiful setting lends itself to create a 'special experience' for campers. The clifftop field is a perfect setting to watch the sunset or moon reflect off the water at night. The facilities are basic but very clean. No EHU.

FACILITIES...
TOILETS
SHOWERS
DOG FRIENDLY
WASTE DISPOSAL

PORTHIAGO CAMPSITE
RHOSHIRWAUN, GWYNEDD, LL53 8LP | 07415 455010

The dream location for a campsite! Overlooking the unbelievably beautiful Porth Iago beach which has some of the most incredible sunsets. The facilities are basic but clean. You'll be hard pushed to find a more tranquil and picturesque setting for a campsite.

FACILITIES...
TOILETS
SHOWERS
DOG FRIENDLY
WASTE DISPOSAL

HOTELS, BNB'S AND ACCOMMODATION

THE CAERWYLAN | £££
BEACHBANK, CRICCIETH, LL52 0HW | 01766 522547

4 Star hotel with incredible ratings set in landmark Victorian building overlooking some of the best seaside views on the Llyn Peninsula. Booking online in advance is advisable.

PORTH TOCYN | £££
BWLCHTOCYN, ABERSOCH, PWLLHELI, LL53 7BU | 01758 713303

Porth Tocyn is a traditional and timeless, family run hotel, in a stunning coastal location. It has a heated outdoor pool and lovely bedrooms. Dog friendly hotel.

AWAY FROM IT ALL - GLAMPING | ££-£££
PENFRAS ISAF, LLWYNDYRYS, LL53 6NG | 01758 750279

Unique glamping in dome tents, a converted horsebox or a former pigsty - what's not to love about these random mix of options? Great location definitely worth checking out!

TOP TIP

VISIT THE TY COCH INN, ONE OF THE MOST AMAZING PUB LOCATIONS!

WHISTLING SANDS

WHERE TO EAT & DRINK

TONNAU RESTAURANT | BRITISH & LOCALLY SOURCED
BEACH BANK, CRICCIETH, LL52 0HW

NO. 46 COFFEE SHOP | TEA, COFFEE & SNACKS
46 HIGH STREET, CRICCIETH, LL52 0E

SBLASH FISH BAR | GREAT FISH AND CHIPS
ABERDARON, PWLLHELI, LL53 8BE

TŶ COCH INN | SIMPLE FOOD, GREAT BEER, AMAZING LOCATION
PORTHDINLLAEN, MORFA NEFYN, PWLLHELI, LL53 6DB

FOLLOW ME ON INSTAGRAM

I POST PHOTOS AND TRAVEL TIPS ON MY INSTAGRAM AND FACEBOOK PAGE REGULARLY! GO AND FOLLOW ME...

INSTAGRAM - @ROBBIEROAMS
FACEBOOK - ROBBIE ROAMS

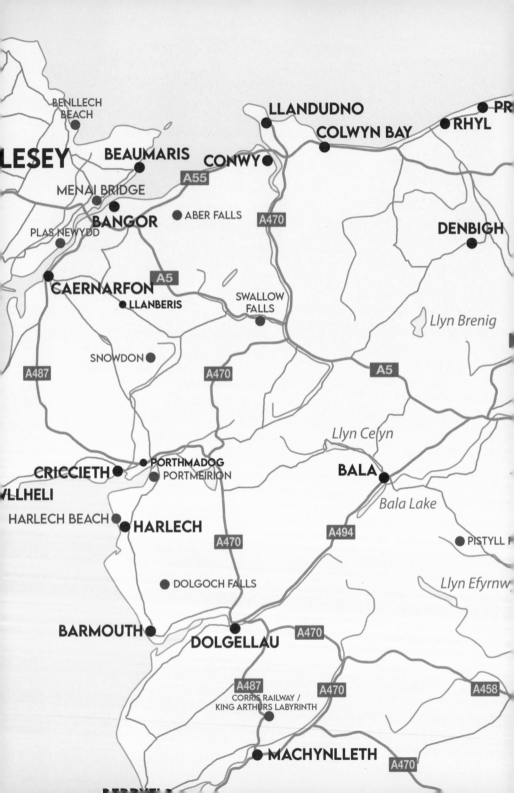

SNOWDONIA

ON THE ROAD IN SNOWDONIA

SNOWDONIA

SNOWDON MOUNTAIN RAILWAY

THIS PLACE IS TRULY BREATHTAKING!

The incredible Snowdonia National Park is home to the mighty Snowdon - the highest mountain in Wales. Packed with rugged mountainous landscapes, spectacular waterfalls and epic castles, Snowdonia must been seen to be believed. It's ideal for adrenaline junkies, hikers and those who really love the outdoors.

MUST SEES...

LLANBERIS
SNOWDON
WATKIN PATH
WATERFALLS
HARLECH BEACH
BARMOUTH

THINGS TO SEE AND DO...

LLANBERIS & THE LLANBERIS PASS

LLANBERIS,
LL55 4TY
///BLOGS.REGION.TUNED

The gateway to Snowdon! Llanberis is a charming village set on lake Llyn Padarn and at the foot of Snowdon. It's home to the Snowdon Mountain Railway, Llanberis Railway and The National Slate Musuem. The iconic 13th century Dolbadarn Castle stands proudly above the village. Driving the Llanberis Pass is breath taking and a must do on your Welsh road trip! Simply drive from Llanberis towards Pen-y-Pass and you'll be surrounded by the impressive Snowdon mountains to the right and the Glyderau mountains to the left.

NATIONAL SLATE MUSEUM
LLANBERIS,
LL55 4TY
///SMILING.BUMP.
BLEACHING

Shadowed by towering slate mountains, the National Slate Museum Llanberis is housed in the Industrial Victorian Workshops that once serviced and maintained the enormous Dinorwig slate quarry above it. The museum is free to enter (great for a rainy day) and is open year round apart from Saturdays from November to Easter.

SNOWDON
LL55 4NU
///SUPER.ULTRA.
ENHANCEMENT

The highest mountain in Wales standing at a whopping 1,085 metres. Snowdon dominates the skies of Snowdonia and is a hikers paradise! With six main walking paths up and down the mountain, Snowdon is one of the UK's most popular mountain climbs. Having previously climbed the mountain a few times, I can tell you it's not a walk in the park, but if you have a relative level of fitness it shouldn't be a problem. (If climbing a mountain sounds like a day from hell, read the next paragraph – you can actually catch a train up and down). On a clear day the views are absolutely spectacular! The Pyg and Miners track offer the most scenic views – perhaps ascend up The Pyg and descend down the Miners? The Llanberis path is the easiest for beginners. Always remember to check the weather, avoid climbing in snow and ice and wear suitable warm and waterproof clothing.

SNOWDON MOUNTAIN RAILWAY
LLANBERIS,
LL55 4TU
///COMMUNITY.COASTER.
FLOPS

If you're short on time or really don't fancy the hike up Snowdon then you're in luck! The Snowdon Mountain Railway, described as one of the most scenic railway journeys in the world, will take you all the way up to the summit. You can book a return journey or a single allowing you to hike back down the mountain. The railway is open from mid-March until the end of October and return tickets are approximately £35 Adults / £25 Children. Always book in advance online – the railway is popular and has limited timings.

WATKIN PATH WATERFALLS
(PARKING)
NANT GWYNANT,
LL55 4NH
///ACCLAIM.SEAWEED.
STILTED

Follow the Watkin Path towards the summit of Snowdon for around 25-30 minutes and you'll reach a set of magnificent waterfalls. Cross over a small bridge to find some of the best falls which lead into deep pools of turquoise blue water, perfect for plunging into on a warm day. It's hard to believe the water is so clear and blue! I had a dip here on my last trip, what an experience!

WATKIN PATH WATERFALLS

ABER FALLS

ZIPWORLD
MULTIPLE LOCATIONS
(PENRHYN QUARRY)
BETHESDA, BANGOR,
LL57 4YG
///STUFF.COURTS.DAMPEN

With multiple locations around North Wales, Zip World is the ultimate day out for adrenaline junkies. From the worlds fastest zipline taking you over Penrhyn Quarry at over 100mph or the UK's only alpine coaster at the Zip World Fforest. They have multiple activities to get the heart racing. I can confirm the velocity 2 zipline is bloody fantastic, if not a little scary. Book ahead online.

BETWS-Y-COED
LL24 0AH
///SADDENS.WORTH.GONG

Buzzing Betws-y-Coed is the gateway to the snowy peaks and dazzling lakes of Snowdonia National Park. This magical setting has a distinctly Alpine feel enhanced by the dense Gwydyr Forest surrounding Betws-y-Coed. The quaint village is very photogenic so don't forget to take a few snaps when passing through.

RHAEADR EWYNNOL SWALLOW FALLS
BETWS-Y-COED,
LL24 0DW
///BLOWS.GIFTED.BOLSTERS

A must do if you're in the area. This majestic waterfall on the Afon Llugwy has plenty of parking nearby and is open year round. It's close to Betws-Y-Coed and costs just £2 for adults and £1 for children using coins or contactless. You can view the falls from both the top and bottom.

ABER FALLS
ABERGWYNGREGYN,
LLANFAIRFECHAN,
LL33 0LP
///ULTERIOR.FLATTERY.
HOAXES

A jaw dropping 120ft waterfall set in a wonderful Welsh valley accessed by an easy 4km walk (there and back). I thoroughly enjoyed exploring Aber Falls with Archie and actually wished I'd have brought my swimming shorts to have a dip in one of the pools at the bottom. If you're looking for a peaceful way to stretch your legs, this place is perfect. The path to access Aber Falls is highly accessible for wheelchairs and prams. Located between Conwy and Bangor at the Northern tip of Snowdonia.

PORTHMADOG
LL49 9EH
///DEPLOYED.SPANS.
UNSCREW

A scenic harbour town that was once a busy local slate port. These days, Porthmadog is an ideal base for tourism and exploring Snowdonia. The Ffestiniog Railway takes you on a 13 1/2-mile journey from the harbour in Porthmadog to the slate-quarrying town of Blaenau Ffestiniog. It is also recognised as the oldest railway company in the world being founded in 1832. Nearby is the stunning Black Rock Sands Beach and within the town is a number of local shops & supermarkets (Tesco & Lidl - ideal for stocking up).

@ROBBIEROAMS

PORTMEIRION

PORTMEIRION
PENRHYNDEUDRAETH,
LL48 6ET
///PUDDLES.ACTOR.
SOLUTIONS

Built by Sir Clough William-Ellis in the style of an Italian village, Portmeirion (pictured on page 107) is an 'enchanting village' overlooking stunning North Wales coastal scenery. The unique tourist village & gardens makes for a great morning or afternoon visit. Entry prices are £17.00 for adults and £10.00 for children although dogs aren't allowed within the grounds.

BLACK ROCK SANDS BEACH
MORFA BYCHAN,
PORTHMADOG,
LL49 9YH
///STAR.CROUTONS.
LOCATING

Also known as Traeth y Greigddu. A beautiful wide beach with fine sands backed by dunes, interesting rock formations, caves and you can even park up right on the beach. If you're in a motorhome or campervan, it's an ideal place to pitch up for the day!

HARLECH BEACH
HARLECH,
LL46 2PU
///TRICKLED.MEANING.
ROBOTS

This beach is special! Flat white sand, stunning dunes and it's a long one (stretching for 4 miles). If you're heading North on the A496 you'll get a magnificent view right over the bay (if you're heading South towards Barmouth you'll also get chance to look back at its beauty). Harlech beach sits right alongside the world famous Royal St. David's Golf Club and is in close proximity to Harlech Castle. If you stay at Shell Island or Barmouth, Harlech beach is a must see!

HARLECH CASTLE
HARLECH,
LL46 2YH
///ROOST.CRUMPLE.ALBUM

A UNESCO World Heritage Site! What more can I say? Harlech Castle is a mediaeval Fort built in the 13th century overlooking the Irish Sea. Harlech Castle is open year round and along with Beaumaris, Conwy, and Caernarfon, is thought to be one of *"the finest examples of late 13th century and early 14th century military architecture in Europe"*. Against fierce competition from Conwy, Caernarfon and Beaumaris, this is probably the most spectacular setting for any of Edward I's castles in North Wales.

COUNTING CASTLES

HOW MANY OF KING EDWARD I'S CASTLES WILL YOU VISIT ON YOUR WELSH ROAD TRIP? THERE ARE 4 IN TOTAL, ALL ARE SPECTACULAR!

SHELL ISLAND
LLANBEDR,
LL45 2PJ
///DISTORTS.BULGES.TRIBAL

One of Europe's largest campsites, Shell Island is a massive 300-acre campsite located in unspoiled countryside with beautiful beaches, scenic sand dunes and it even has a pub on-site. Camping here is unique in that you can find your own pitch anywhere on the site. The views out to sea are really special and if you aren't camping, you can visit for the day.

BARMOUTH
LL42 1LX
///BUCKET.DRILLING.
MATCHBOX

A charming seaside town with a large beach, quaint harbour and delicious fish, chips & ice cream! Barmouth has a little bit of something for everyone. There are boat trips from the harbour, amusements for the kids and quirky independent shops for a mooch around. If you're staying at Shell Island or need to pick up supplies for your road trip, there is a Co-op conveniently located in the center of the town. I'd highly recommend a stop at Knickerbockers Ice Cream Parlor – did you really go to Barmouth if you didn't get an ice cream?

BALA (LLYN TEGID)
LL23 7SW
///SUMMIT.SPILL.FUNNELS

Known as Llyn Tegid in Welsh, Lake Bala is Wales' largest natural lake. Enjoy a 9 mile return journey on the Bala Lake Railway where you can take in views of Snowdonia and the lake itself. Lake Bala also has a number of outdoor activities on offer including kayaking, climbing and gorge walking. The historic market town of Bala is also worth a visit.

DOLGOCH FALLS
TYWYN, LL36 9UW
///HOBBIT.RELIEVES.SEND

A short and well signposted walk of around 1 mile (round trip) will present a series of falls located in a picturesque forest ravine. The trail is generally easy and will pass several caves along the way. Located just 18 minutes from Aberdovey (Aderdyfi) and just 20 minutes away from Machynlleth, Dolgoch falls is a lovely stop off if you happen to find yourself in South West Snowdonia.

ABERDOVEY /
ABERDYFI
LL35 0EA
///PROPOSE.DISHED.
HEADBOARD

Located on the Northern Side of the River Dyfi estuary, Aberdovey is a 'thriving little harbour resort' popular for its numerous watersports, award winning beach stretching for over 3 miles and its championship golf course. The houses sat behind the harbour, described as 'cute' by Jasmin, are painted in different colors and make for a nice postcard photo.

SHELL ISLAND CAMPSITE

WHERE TO STAY...

CAMPING, MOTORHOMES AND CARAVANS

SHELL ISLAND CAMPSITE
LLANBEDR, LL45 2PJ | 01341 241 453

A stunning campsite set over 300 acres of unspoiled countryside, beaches and sand dunes. I've had so many memorable trips here over the years and being able to find you own pitch within the sand dunes or overlooking the sea is brilliant. The facilities are good with an onsite pub, restaurant and shop. No EHU. Highly recommended from me! Book ahead in the summer months, it's a popular place.

FACILITIES...
TOILETS
SHOWERS
DOG FRIENDLY
WASTE DISPOSAL

LLYN GWYNANT CAMPSITE
NANT GWYNANT, LL55 4NW | 01766 890302

Back to nature camping in the heart of the Snowdonia National Park, beside mountain, river and lake – a perfect Snowdon base camp. Very peaceful surrounded by huge mountains. Close to the Watkin Path. Lovely place to stay in Snowdownia.

FACILITIES...
ELECTRIC HOOK UP
TOILETS
SHOWERS
DOG FRIENDLY
WASTE DISPOSAL

HOTELS, BNB'S AND ACCOMMODATION

DOLAFON GUEST HOUSE | ££-£££
HIGH STREET, LLANBERIS, LL55 4SU | 01286 870993

Exceptional ratings and the perfect base to explore Snowdon, Llanberis and Snowdonia. Minimum 2 night stay and only 5 minute walk to the Dolbadarn Castle.

DOLFFANOG FAWR | £££
TAL-Y-LLYN, LL36 9AJ | 01654 761247

An 18th Century farmhouse that has recently been thoroughly renovated and converted into one of the finest small luxury bed and breakfast guest houses in Snowdonia.

BRYN DINAS PODS | ££-£££
NANT GWYNANT, LL55 4NH | 01766 890351

Stay in cottages, lodges, log cabins or camping pods set in privately owned mountainside woodland just 300 metres from the start of the Snowdon Watkin Path.

TOP TIP

STAY AT THE UNIQUE SHELL ISLAND CAMSPITE, REMARKABLE SURROUNDINGS!

BARMOUTH

WHERE TO EAT & DRINK

CAFFI GWYNANT | BREAKFAST OR LUNCH (NEAR SNOWDON)
NANT GWYNANT, LL55 4NH

CELTIC CABIN | TASTY BEACHSIDE WRAPS & QUESADILLAS
THE PROMENADE, BARMOUTH, LL42 1HW

Y SGWAR | FANTASTIC LUNCH AND DINNER
12-16 MARKET SQUARE, TREMADOG, PORTHMADOG, LL49 9RB

GWYNDY TEAROOMS & SHOP | TEA, COFFEE, LUNCH
GWYNDY BRIDGE STREET, LL40 1AU

HIKING SNOWDON DURING THE PANDEMIC

It was April 2021 and the government had relaxed the COVID-19 rules to allow travel to other areas of the UK. Me and my nut job mates decided we'd go and make the most of it by spending a day hiking up Snowdon. With a few days to go, the weather wasn't looking good and there was still ice at the summit. Remarkably, the day before we were due to visit, the UK randomly had a day of 20 degree sunshine (thanks global warming). So we arrived at Pen-Y-Pass and set off bright and early. Our plan was to climb the Pyg track and come back down the Miners track. Apart from all of us being completely unfit and struggling for most of the way up, the hike to the summit was game changing for us! We fell in love with Snowdon and its beautiful lakes, peaks and landscapes. Not only that, Snowdon brought out a new found love of hiking which we've since tried to keep up every now and then (Ben Nevis, Scaffel Pike & Pen Y Fan trips subsequently followed). It's a tough slog to get up there, but it sure is worth the effort. Snowdon is spectacular and a must do if you are able.

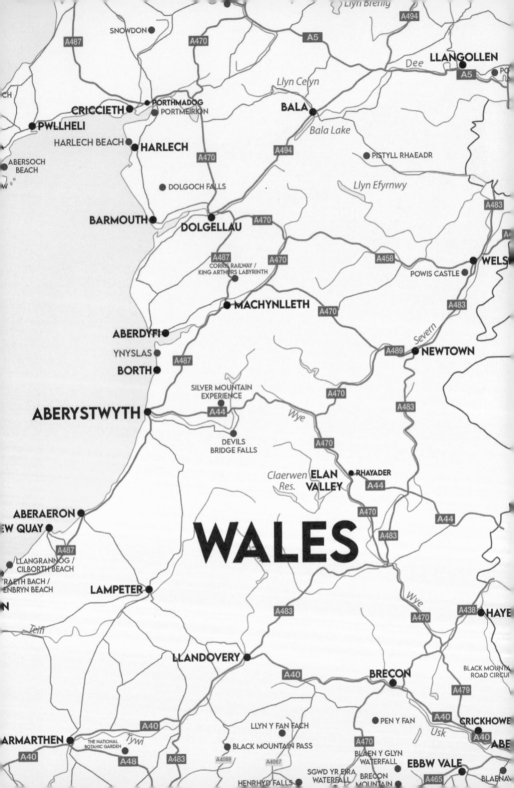

ABERYSTWYTH & MID WALES

ABERYSTWYTH

ABERYSTWYTH & MID WALES

YNYSLAS

THE BEATING HEART OF WALES!

The skies are filled with red kites, the seas are filled with dolphins and the towns are filled with friendly smiling faces. I did come up with that myself (go me). Seriously though, Mid Wales is a special part of the country that offers a range of diverse countryside, coastline and mountains. There is a lot to love.

MUST SEES...

BORTH & YNYSLAS
ABERYSTWYTH
POWIS CASTLE
ELAN VALLEY
ABERAERON
NEW QUAY

THINGS TO SEE AND DO...

MACHYNLLETH
SY20 8DT
///EPIC.REJECTED.STILTED

A market town and former ancient capital of Wales known as the *'town with the clock'*. Machynlleth hosts the 'Wednesday market' which has been going for 700 years and is also home to the Machynlleth Comedy Festival taking place over the May Bank Holiday each year. There are a number of things to do nearby including the highly rated *'Falconry Experience Wales'* where you have the opportunity to fly and handle a variety of birds of prey. Why not try your hand at falconry? Who knows, it could be your new hobby? (Pardon the pun).

KING ARTHURS LABYRINTH
UNIT 11, CORRIS CRAFT CENTRE, CORRIS, SY20 9RF
///AWARD.CORRECTS. CROUCHES

Located just north of Machynlleth in Corris – King Arthurs Labyrinth is an underground storytelling adventure where you sail through a magical waterfall and deep into the mountains of Southern Snowdonia. Ideal for a rainy day escape, the attraction is great for children (double check opening times before visiting).

CORRIS RAILWAY
STATION YARD, MACHYNLLETH. SY20 9SH
///CUSTARD.BRINK.BOOT

Another attraction located near to Machynlleth is the enjoyable Corris Steam Railway which offers riders a gentle trip down the beautiful Dulas valley. Tickets are £8.00 for Adults and £4.00 for Children (5-15 years).

BORTH & YNYSLAS
SY24 5JX
///FADE.SLICE.HARDBACK

Borth is a village and seaside resort just 7 miles north of Aberystwyth. It has a solid range of shops, cafes, restaurants and pubs to match its fantastic beach. Just 1.5 miles to the north is the magnificent Ynyslas Beach & Dyif National Nature Reserve. If the weather is on side, Ynyslas is one of them spectacular locations that wouldn't be out of place on a postcard from Australia or any other tropical location (minus the palm trees of course). I have fond memories of swimming in the sea here as a kid with our old collie Jess. Parking at Ynyslas is super easy. Across the Dyfi esturary is the town of Aberdyfi (Aberdovey) and although it may seem close, it will actually take you around 45 minutes in the car!

ABERYSTWYTH
SY23 2EG
///TRADER.NOVEL. UNSECURED

A university seaside town in Ceredigion, Aberystwyth is a must visit west coast location! I have a real soft spot for Aber having spent many school holidays here as a kid! The town centre has a wealth of shops, cafes, pubs & restaurants and has two main beaches. Exploring the town is easy so long as you can find a parking space on or near to the promenade which isn't a guarantee on a busy day or weekend. A trip up to Constitution Hill via the Aberystwyth Cliff Railway (dogs welcome) will provide excellent views across the town and over to the nearby Clarach Bay in the other direction. Hike up to Pen Dinas Hill Fort for more exquisite views over the town and surrounding valleys. Fish and chips is a must from either the Pier or the chippy opposite!

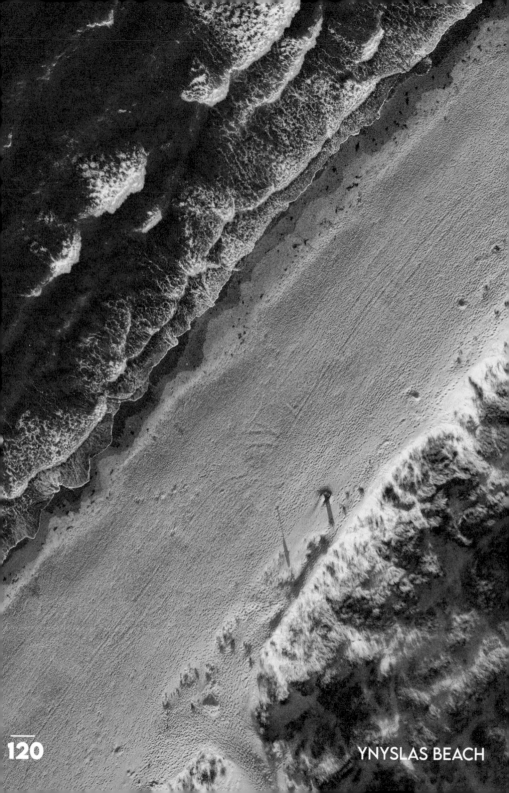

YNYSLAS BEACH

PEN DINAS HILL FORT

VALE OF RHEIDOL RAILWAY
PARK AVE,
ABERYSTWYTH,
SY23 1PG
///PROTECTED.FACTORING.
FACTORING

An unforgettable 12 mile journey from Aberystwyth to the breathtaking Devil's Bridge on a steam railway journey that will take you up 700ft through some of Mid-Wales' most spectacular scenery. This is obviously great for kids and adults alike. I have great childhood memories of the Rheidol railway! Return tickets are priced at £33.00 for Adults, £2.75 for Children (aged 3 to 15) and Dogs are £4.00.

DEVILS BRIDGE FALLS
PONTARFYNACH,
ABERYSTWYTH,
SY23 3JW
///LOOPS.BRACELET.RULES

A stunning set of waterfalls and trails in the Cambrian Mountains just 12 miles from Aberystwyth. The falls can be accessed via the Vale of Rheidol Railway or there is free parking is available at the falls. There are two main trails available. The Nature Trail Walk will take 45mins to 1 hour with 675 steps (some are very steep) and tickets will cost £4.00 Adults & £2.50 for Children. The alternate 'Punch Bowl Walk' offers a shorter route to the falls taking around 20 to 30 minutes in total with entry via a coin-operate turnstile for £2.00 per person (bring coins with you). For me, Devils Bridge Falls are a must see if you're in or around the area! I absolutely love this place.

BWLCH NANT YR ARIAN FOREST VISITOR CENTRE
PONTERWYD,
ABERYSTWYTH,
SY23 3AB
///FOLLOW.PLAYFULLY.
CLASPING

An ideal stop off to stretch your legs and breath in some of the wonderful Welsh mountain air! The main attraction is the Red Kite feeding which takes place as 3pm every day. Follow a short trail to the main viewing area where you'll be able to get the best views of the kite feeding spectacle! It really is a unique and worthwhile experience that can easily be tied in with a trip to Devils Bridge Falls (just 10 minutes away) and the Silver Mountain Experience (just 1 mile away). There's a visitor centre, café and shop open daily.

SILVER MOUNTAIN EXPERIENCE
PONTERWYD,
ABERYSTWYTH,
SY23 3AB
///SHARPEN.PUTTER.
VANDALISM

A unique guided experience which immerses you in the original and rare setting of the 250+ year old Silver-Lead Mine. You can explore Welsh myth & legend with 3 different actor led experiences. There are also escape rooms, an onsite café and the Halloween event – Terror Mountain where you can scare yourself silly during certain dates in October!

DEVILS BRIDGE FALLS

WELSHPOOL
SY21 7RZ
///PUDDINGS.NOTCHED.
TENDER

A perfect base for exploring the beautiful sights of Mid Wales. This market town in Powys has a number of attractions nearby including the Rhiw Valley Light Railway, Welshpool & Llanfair Light Railway, Montgomery Canal, Powysland Musuem and the iconic Powis Castle. Welshpool has several major supermarkets should you need to stock up on any supplies.

POWIS CASTLE & GARDEN
WELSHPOOL,
SY21 8RF
///MASTERING.MAGNUM.
REMEMBERS

A world-famous garden, 13th century medieval castle and extensive historic collection. Powis Castle was built around 1200 as a fortress sitting high on a rock above its world-famous garden which is influenced by Italian and French styles. It has one of the UK's most significant collections of Indian objects displayed in the Clive Museum at the castle. Powis Castle & Garden has many themed events throughout the year (some of which are free) and standard tickets from the National Trust are priced at £14.00 for Adults and £7.00 for Children.

NEWTOWN
SY16 1BP
///ROOST.CRUMPLE.ALBUM

Located on the banks of the River Severn and despite having history routed back to the 13th century, Newtown was designated a 'new town' in 1967. It lies not far from the Wales-England border with Welshpool just 20 minutes to the north and Rhayader & The Elan Valley 40 minutes to the south. Follow the Newtown Heritage Trail for a fascinating journey 'through the ages.'. The Newtown Textile Museum is highly rated and if you're looking for something a little more off-piste, visit Beyond Breakout escape rooms.

RHAYADER
LD6 5AL
///NOOKS.AMENDING.
SPROUTS

Home to the spectacular dams and reservoirs of the Elan and Claerwen Valleys, Rhayader is a market town in Powys branded as 'the adventure capital of Wales'. Located 20 miles from the source of the River Wye, Rhayader has a number of tea rooms, shops, pubs & restaurants to enjoy within its charming town centre. Rhayader's famous landmark is the Rhayader War Memorial Clock Tower located in the centre of town. It was unveiled in 1924 as a memorial to the local people who died in the First World War. Names of those who died in the Second World War were added later.

 @ROBBIEROAMS

GIGRIN FARM RED KITE FEEDING CENTRE
SOUTH ST,
RHAYADER,
LD6 5BL
///COLDER.EDICTS.
PRINTOUT

A 160 acre family-run working farm which is now famous for its Red Kite Feeding Centre where you can witness hundreds of Red Kites in a 'breath-taking' spectacle. Get your camera ready! A family ticket is £25 (2 Adults & 2 Children) and individual tickets are priced at £9.00 for Adults & £5.00 for children (ages 4-15).

ELAN VALLEY
RHAYADER,
LD6 5HS
///BUCKET.DRILLING.
MATCHBOX

As part of the Cambrian Mountains, Elan is a beautiful and relatively unspoiled area that draws visitors year round because of its dams and reservoirs which make for a dramatic landscape. Any budding photographers or stargazers will be at home here as it has International Dark Sky Park status. The 45,000 acres of Elan Valley are protected against light pollution, so you'll be in awe of the stars on a clear night!

ELAN VALLEY TRAIL
RHAYADER,
LD6 5HS
///BUCKET.DRILLING.
MATCHBOX

With its breathtaking landscapes, the Elan Valley trail is a hidden gem located in the very heart of Wales. This linear trail takes you past three reservoirs and can be followed in either direction, but most people head west from Cwmdeuddwr towards the valley. The total route is 14km and will take around 3 hours to complete. Don't forget to bring your camera or phone to photograph some of the scenic dams and landscapes. This trail is superb for dog walking!

ELAN VALLEY

ABERAERON
SA46 0HZ
///IDEALS.PUPPETS.HARDER

A 30 minute drive south from Aberystwyth will lead you to the enchanting town of Aberaeron. Its crown jewels are the charming colorful houses and as a location it's ideal for a mooch around the harbour, exploring the shops and enjoying a spot of lunch on the water's edge. It's not a huge place so perhaps an hour or two will do the job. Foodies should definitely go for the fresh fish options here! Although I'm not a seafood fan, Aberaeron is known for it! The Stubborn Duckling, The Cellar (Y Seler) and The Hive are just a few tasty places to check out.

NEW QUAY
SA45 9NR
///INTRUDING.BEDROOMS.PLANKTON

Not to be confused with the Newquay in Cornwall, New Quay, West Wales is a real gem! It has so much to offer with its picturesque harbour, beautiful sandy beaches and its fantastic pubs, cafes & shops which are set on a sloping hill. On a sunny day you could convince yourself you were in Cornwall it really does have that kind of vibe! As one of the best places to spot Dolphins in the whole of the UK, New Quay has a number of wildlife boat trips leaving the harbour each day. On our last visit here the sun was shining, the beach was buzzing and we loved soaking up the friendly atmosphere with a pasty from 'Pasty Pasty' whilst sinking an ice cold pint from The Blue Bell.

LLANGRANNOG & CILBORTH BEACHES
LLANDYSUL,
SA44 6SN
///DENIM.LIKES.EYELINER

This part of Cardigan bay has so many picture perfect sandy beaches (I didn't have room to write about them all). The picturesque village of Llangrannog nestles in the narrow valley behind the beach and has a seafront car park, a shop and a couple of pubs and cafes. The pretty hidden beach at Cilborth is accessible from Llangrannog either at low tide across the beach or via steep steps on the coastal path. Dogs are allowed at both beaches.

TOP TIP

BOOK ONTO A BOAT TRIP FROM NEW QUAY TO SPOT DOLPHINS AND OTHER WILDLIFE! YOU MUST ALSO TRY A PASTY FROM 'PASTY PASTY' IN NEW QUAY, SUPER DELICIOUS!

TRAETH BACH & PENBRYN BEACH
LLANDYSUL,
SA44 6RS
LD6 5BL
///REGAL.SPILLING.
HEARTENED

Located on the fabulous coastal path just a mile or so apart, these two beaches are simply stunning. If you head down to Traeth Bach (which means little beach in Welsh) you'll probably have it to yourself or perhaps share it with a few people at most. Unfortunately, it's difficult to access via a steep path (start at the Penbryn National Trust car park and head north along the cliff top). The path isn't suitable for children or anyone with mobility issues so please take care. Penbryn Beach described as *'one of Ceredigion's best-kept secrets'* is more accessible with a drop off point for disabled visitors and offers a lovely woodland walk from the car park. Dogs aren't allowed here between May and September. The Plwmp Tart café is the place to go for a lunch time snack.

ABERPORTH BEACH
ABERPORTH,
CARDIGAN,
SA43 2DB
///PLAYING.DOWNFIELD.
REJOICED

Aberporth is known for being a charming little village on the coast of Ceredigion and Aberporth Beach (split in two) is one of the prettiest in the area. With a gentle slope, this sandy beach is perfect for a swim or paddle. Aberpoth has several rock pools to explore at low tide (great for kids) and dogs are allowed at 1 of the 2 beaches. Parking can be problematic in the busier summer months.

MWNT BEACH
SA43 1QH
///RECLINE.RESET.IMPLORE

A truly beautiful hidden cove on the Ceredigion coast! This place made my jaw drop and if you decide to visit here, you'll see the reason why! Managed by the National Trust, Mwnt Beach is off the beaten track but because of its sheer beauty, is very popular during the summer months so arrive early to bag a decent spot or perhaps come later in the day when it starts to become quieter. If you don't fancy a beach day or aren't up for making the relatively steep walk down to the beach then don't worry, the views from the top of the hill are magnificent! This blue flag beach has a seasonal take away café and is one of the best places for dolphin spotting. Dogs aren't allowed between May and September unfortunately, but, I would still call in just to get a glimpse of this marvelous bay. I'm glad I accidentally stumbled across this place on my last Wales road trip, what a cracker!

ROBBIEROAMS.COM

CARDIGAN
SA43 1JA
///KENNELS.WRIST.KEEPERS

The gateway to the Teifi Valley, this ancient town sits at the base of Cardigan Bay near the border with Pembrokeshire. Cardigan Island Coastal Farm Park is a great shout for children and offers stunning views over the coast. Cardigan Castle sits near the town centre which is home to some great eateries including The Copper Pot, Crowes and Crwst.

CARDIGAN ISLAND COASTAL FARM PARK
GWBERT,
CARDIGAN,
SA43 1PR
///EASED.PURSE.HOOPS

Named for its spectacular views across to Cardigan Island just 200 metres offshore, this unique Farm Park which also overlooks the Teifi estuary and Pembrokeshire Coast National Park, is located on a picturesque headland in the southern part of Cardigan Bay. The island itself is a private nature reserve owned by The Wildlife Trust of South and West Wales. Say hello to the farm animals; enjoy the fenced clifftop walk to the headland from where you can watch seals in the wild that breed in the caves below the Farm Park cliffs or spot frequent dolphin visitors. With play areas for children, a cafe and a campsite, the Cardigan Island Coastal Farm Park could be a very good idea!

POPPIT SANDS BEACH
ST DOGMAELS,
CARDIGAN,
SA43 3LR
///DATED.JETLINER.MIXERS

The official start (or end) of the Pembrokeshire coastal path, Poppit Sands is a very accessible long sandy beach backed with sand dunes and is dog friendly. There are toilets, taps for filling dog bowls and the beach is manned by lifeguards in the summer months. The café is also highly rated should you work up an appetite on this lovely huge beach.

CARDIGAN RIVER & FOOD FESTIVAL

TAKING PLACE IN AUGUST EVERY YEAR – THE CARDIGAN RIVER & FOOD FESTIVAL IS A COMMUNITY REGENERATION PROJECT THAT WELCOMES THE BEST INDEPENDENT FOOD & DRINK PRODUCERS THAT WALES HAS TO OFFER. THERE ARE ALSO BANDS AND LIVE PERFORMERS!

@ROBBIEROAMS – FIND ME ON INSTAGRAM

MWNT BEACH

WHERE TO STAY...

CAMPING, MOTORHOMES AND CARAVANS

TŶ-GWYN CAMPSITE
YNYSLAS, BORTH, SY24 5LA | 01970 871894

Ideal location just 300 yards from Ynyslas beach! A small, family run campsite with basic but clean facilites. Worth it for the location.

FACILITIES...
TOILETS
SHOWERS
DOG FRIENDLY
WASTE DISPOSAL

ELAN OAKS - CAMPING & CARAVAN SITE
ELAN VALLEY, RHAYADER, LD6 5HP | 01597 810326

Based at the entrance to the beautiful Elan Valley. With direct access to this awe-inspiring estate, less than 2 miles from Rhayader.

FACILITIES...
ELECTRIC HOOK UP
TOILETS / SHOWERS
DOG FRIENDLY
WASTE DISPOSAL

SEVERN CARAVAN PARK
WELSHPOOL, SY21 8RT | 01938 580238

Beautiful site adjacent to the River Severn, the place to stay for friendly, comfortable and affordable accommodation.

FACILITIES...
ELECTRIC HOOK UP
TOILETS / SHOWERS
DOG FRIENDLY
WASTE DISPOSAL

TŶ GWYN CARAVAN AND CAMPING PARK
MWNT, CARDIGAN, SA43 1QH | 01766 890302

Within walking distance of Mwnt beach, the camping park overlooks Cardigan Bay where dolphins and seals can regularly be found and has direct access to the Wales coastal path.

FACILITIES...
ELECTRIC HOOK UP
TOILETS
SHOWERS
DOG FRIENDLY
WASTE DISPOSAL

HOTELS, BNB'S AND ACCOMMODATION

NANTEOS MANSION | £££
RHYDYFELIN, ABERYSTWYTH, SY23 4LU | 01970 600522
Luxury Country House Hotel situated in 30 acres of wooded parkland.

THE ELAN HOTEL | ££-£££
WEST ST, RHAYADER, LD6 5AF | 01597 811208
Straightforward rooms with free parking and cooked breakfast near to Elan Valley.

BLACK LION HOTEL | ££-£££
NEW QUAY, SA45 9PT | 01545 560122
Overlooks the bay just minutes walk down to the harbour. Welsh breakfast included.

THE GWBERT HOTEL | ££-£££
CORONATION DR, GWBERT, CARDIGAN, SA43 1PP | 01239 612638
4 star hotel on the banks of the River Teifi. One of the finest hotels in the area.

PENBRYN BEACH

WHERE TO EAT & DRINK

LITTLE ITALY | HIGHLY RATED ITALIAN
51 NORTH PARADE, ABERYSTWYTH, SY23 2JN

DYFFRYN CAFE & RESTAURANT | EXCELLENT ROAD SIDE EATERY
A458, WELSHPOOL, SY21 0NU

THE TRIANGLE INN | GOOD HONEST PUB FOOD
CWMDAUDDWR, RHAYADER, LD6 5AR

PASTY PASTY | FRESH PASTIES, BAKES AND MORE
SOUTH JOHN STREET, NEW QUAY, SA45 9NP

CHILDHOOD MEMORIES OF YNYSLAS...

One of the most vivid childhood memories I have of this area involved a fantastic day out at Ynyslas beach. We were lucky to stay at my grandparents static caravan in Aberystwyth during the school holidays quite often and on this occasion, both of my parents came down for the weekend. The weather was absolutely scorching so we jumped in the car and headed up to Ynyslas for the day. If you read the section Ynyslas and Borth, then you will already know that this place is a real paradise! When we arrived at Ynyslas we made our way across the board walk through the sand dunes and onto the huge beach. With my mini inflatable dinghy in hand, I ran straight for the water. I was a complete wimp at that age (I think I was about 9 years old) so the dinghy offered safety from whatever was lurking in the sea. As the tide went out, a huge sandbank appeared cutting off a large pool of water from the sea. I remember being sat on my dinghy being pulled across to a desert island like sand bank with our collie dog Jess swimming alongside. It was such a terrific day with fantastic weather. A truly special day in a great location that I don't think I'll ever forget!

133

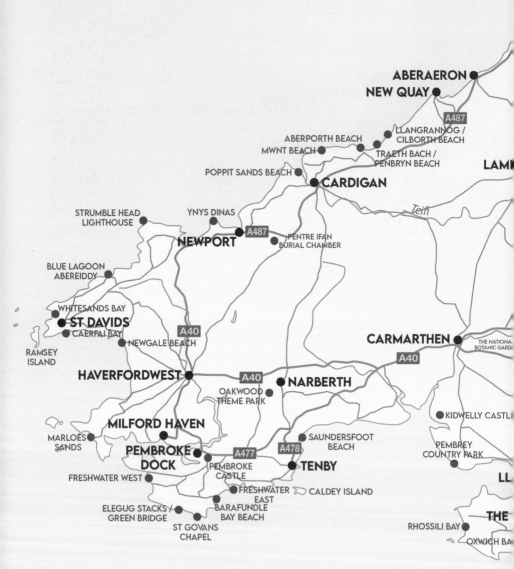

ABERAERON
NEW QUAY
A487

LLANGRANNOG /
CILBORTH BEACH
ABERPORTH BEACH
MWNT BEACH
TRAETH BACH /
PENBRYN BEACH
LAM
POPPIT SANDS BEACH
CARDIGAN
Teifi
STRUMBLE HEAD
LIGHTHOUSE
YNYS DINAS
A487
NEWPORT
PENTRE IFAN
BURIAL CHAMBER
BLUE LAGOON
ABEREIDDY
WHITESANDS BAY
ST DAVIDS
A40
CARMARTHEN
THE NATIONA
BOTANIC GARD
CAERFAI BAY
NEWGALE BEACH
RAMSEY
ISLAND
A40
HAVERFORDWEST
A40
NARBERTH
OAKWOOD
THEME PARK
MILFORD HAVEN
KIDWELLY CASTL
MARLOES
SANDS
PEMBROKE
DOCK
SAUNDERSFOOT
BEACH
PEMBREY
COUNTRY PARK
A477
A478
LL
FRESHWATER WEST
PEMBROKE
CASTLE
TENBY
FRESHWATER
EAST
CALDEY ISLAND
ELEGUG STACKS /
GREEN BRIDGE
BARAFUNDLE
BAY BEACH
THE
ST GOVANS
CHAPEL
RHOSSILI BAY
OXWICH BA

PEMBROKESHIRE

STRUMBLE HEAD LIGHTHOUSE

PEMBROKESHIRE

ST DAVIDS CATHEDRAL

MILES OF AWE-INSPIRING COASTLINE!

This extraordinary corner of South West Wales is rich in dramatic scenery and cultural riches. An area of outstanding natural beauty, you will be amazed by its spectacular coastal features, miles of white sand beaches and the freshest seafood in the whole of Wales. This has quickly become my favourite place to visit!

MUST SEES...

STRUMBLE HEAD

BLUE LAGOON

ST DAVIDS

FRESHWATER WEST

BARAFUNDLE BAY

TENBY

THINGS TO SEE AND DO...

PEMBROKESHIRE COAST PATH

ST DOGMAELS,
CARDIGAN,
SA43 3LR
///MOTELS.DAIRIES.
BRIMMED

The Pembrokeshire Coast Path is a spectacular 186 miles long National Trail covering some of the most varied coastal scenery in Britain, stretching from St Dogmaels in the north to Amroth in the south. Many of the beaches and seaside locations I've included in this guide book are on or near the Coast Path. Now of course, on your road trip you'll probably be following much of the coast via road, but, you should definitely look to complete a section of this incredible path (even just a small section) at some point in your journey.

 @ROBBIEROAMS

PENTRE IFAN BURIAL CHAMBER
NEVERN, CRYMYCH,
SA41 3TZ
///MINGLES.CUPS.PREMIUMS

A striking 5000 year old megalithic monument in located just 10 minutes away from Newport in Pembrokeshire. This prehistoric burial chamber was constructed using rock from the nearby Preseli Hills, the exact same rock used at Stonehenge. It's easy to access and free to visit using the small car park on-site.

NEWPORT & NEWPORT BEACH
SA42 0NR
///STARFISH.ROBOTS.SOUK

DO NOT mix this place up with Newport in South Wales, it's the polar opposite! This small bustling coastal village 'flanked' by a mountain, an estuary and wonderful beaches is a go to place for food-lovers, beach-lovers and explorers. Newport Sands beach ticks all of the necessary boxes including easy access, café & toilets nearby and it is dog friendly.

YNYS DINAS / DINAS ISLAND (DINAS HEAD)
NEWPORT,
SA42 0SE
///ESTIMATED.CROAK.
REVEAL

Dinas Island is a peninsula which is partially detached from the mainland and offers a spectacular circular walk which isn't a particularly long one at 3 miles, but, requires a moderate level of fitness (or a few stops to get your breath back). The walk starts at the Pwllgwaelod car park and offers some of the finest views anywhere on the Pembrokeshire coast. The walk will take around 2 hours and you may be able to spot seals in the some of the small coves along the route. There's a great pub lunch waiting for you after the walk at The Old Sailor (next to the car park).

STRUMBLE HEAD LIGHTHOUSE
PENCAER,
SA64 0JL
///STUMPY.REGULATOR.
SHOWERING

I've seen some lighthouses in my time researching the Scottish Highlands and let me tell you something, Strumble Head is right up there! My photo of this stunning Pembrokeshire landmark actually takes pride of place on the front / back cover of this book. Originally constructed in 1908, the lighthouse sits on St Michael's Island to the west of Fishguard and was built to mark a dangerous stretch of coast for vessels between Ireland and Wales. Any road trip passing through Pembrokeshire **MUST** pass by this breathtaking location. Not only will you be rewarded by incredible views of the lighthouse and coastline, but you may even be able to spot a pod of dolphins. The surrounding cliffs make for a fantastic picnic spot or tea break. Get your phone or camera ready!

PRESELI VENTURE
PARC-Y-NOLE FACH,
MATHRY,
HAVERFORDWEST,
SA62 5HN
///FARMED.RIDER.LIFEBOATS

This part of Pembrokeshire is an adventurer's paradise and the guys at Preseli Venture have all your outdoor pursuits covered. From sea kayaking to coasteering to surfing, why not make your road trip that little bit more memorable with a half or full day activity?

TRAETH LLYFN BEACH
SA62 6DT
///IMPROVING.CONDIMENT.
EXONERATE

Located just over 1 mile from Abereiddy on the Pembrokeshire Coastal Path, Traeth Llyfn is a relatively untouched sandy beach with turquoise blue waters. Accessible only from the coastal path down a set of steep metal stairs, Treath Llyfn has no facilities or lifeguards and I guess that what makes it a little bit more special and isolated. Just be careful when swimming here, the blue waters are inviting but being so exposed there are powerful waves and rip currents. Dogs are welcome but the metal grid style steps are problematic, it was a problem for ours.

BLUE LAGOON / ABEREIDDY
ABEREIDDY,
HAVERFORDWEST,
SA62 6DT
///KIDNEY.LOBBY.
ECONOMIES

I know what you're thinking, it sounds like a destination in French Polynesia or something off a cocktail menu right? Although the waters may not be as warm as French Polynesia, this place is a real spectacle and must be visited whilst you're in the area. So, what exactly is Abereiddy's Blue Lagoon? It's a former slate quarry that was abandoned and flooded which now makes for a stunning location ideal for coasteering, kayaking and taking a plunge into the deep turquoise blue water. There are great views around the clifftop, the Blue Lagoon has a wheelchair friendly path and the Abereiddy beach at which you'll park is also pleasant and dog friendly. Access to the Blue Lagoon is via a path to the right of the beach if you are facing the sea. Will you be brave enough to jump into The Blue Lagoon? (I wasn't – maybe next time).

FANCY COASTEERING?

A UNIQUE ADVENTURE ACTIVITY WHERE YOU WILL BE SEA LEVEL TRAVERSING, ROCK CLIMBING, CLIFF JUMPING AND SWIMMING. GET UP CLOSE TO SOME OF THE WONDERFUL PEMBROKESHIRE WILDLIFE! GO WITH PRESELI VENTURE.

BLUE LAGOON

ST DAVIDS
HAVERFORDWEST,
SA62 6RD
///SPECIAL.HOTELS.
RELATIVES

It's time to explore Britain's smallest city, St Davids in Pembrokeshire. Obviously, the main attraction is the impressive St Davids Cathedral which was constructed in 1181 and further repaired and extended in the 14th century. Visiting the Cathedral is straightforward with a couple of car parks located nearby. It's open 10am-5pm Monday to Saturday and 1pm-3pm on a Sunday and is definitely worth an hour or two of your time. There's a café on site and church services run multiple times per week. Dogs are allowed within the grounds but not inside the cathedral itself. The city of St Davids has many fabulous independent cafes, restaurants and shops that are worth a mooch while you're here.

WHITESANDS BAY
FEIDR CHWECH-ERW,
ST DAVIDS,
SA62 6PS
///CASCADE.DERAILED.
BLANKED

A beautiful soft sandy beach that's overlooked by the imposing craggy hill of Carn Llidi. It's one of the best surfing beaches in Wales and can get busy on a hot summer's day. If you enjoy surfing, bodyboarding or canoeing the best 'break' is at the northern end of the beach. There are good facilities including toilets (bring change or card) and a café. Parking is £5 and may seem expensive if you only intend to stay for a short period.

RAMSEY ISLAND
LLANDYSUL,
SA62 6SL
///PROUD.GIFTS.MAINLY

Located just one mile from St David's head in Pembrokeshire, Ramsey Island is a dramatic location that has cliffs that rise to 120 meters making it the perfect place for breeding seabirds, flocks of choughs and peregrines. From mid-August, Atlantic Grey seals return to the beaches on Ramsey to give birth and mate. The Island is accessible via boat from 1st April to 31st October and boats run 6 days per week. Book your boat in advance from thousandislands.co.uk to enjoy Ramsey Island.

CAERFAI BAY BEACH
ST DAVIDS,
SA62 6QS
///FLAUNTING.REFLECT.HELD

A stunning bay with crystal clear waters that may appear nothing more than a rocky cove at high tide, but when the tide is out, the soft sand is revealed. There's a steep walk down to the beach and back to the car park so it's not the most easily accessible but this is somewhat of a hidden gem! This is known as a popular beach for dog lovers.

NEWGALE BEACH
SA62 6AR
///VACANCIES.DEPEND.
LEGEND

A beach of epic proportion at almost 2 miles long! Newgale is a surfing / kitesurfing hotspot filled with soft sand backed by a huge pebble bank which was formed after a storm in 1859. If you head down to the Southern side of the beach, there are 'walk-though' caves and sheltered bays to explore. There are three car parks along the beach, a surf shop to hire a board from, café and even a pub. The nearby Newgale campsite is perfectly located overlooking the coastline.

MARLOES SANDS
MARLOES AND ST
BRIDES,
SA62 3BH
///STICKY.HARDBACK.
MARRIED

Located on the Marloes Peninsula, this is a hidden gem on the very western edge of Pembrokeshire (a place that not many people visit). The golden sandy beach stretches for over a mile at low tide and has many rockpools and smaller bays to explore. Scenes from the Hollywood film *"Snow White and the Huntsman"* were filmed here in 2011. There is a National Trust car park fairly close to the beach.

MILFORD HAVEN WATERFRONT
MILFORD HAVEN,
SA73 3AH
///UNSIGHTLY.PROMOTING.
TESTS

A town with a rich history linked to fishing, naval dockyards and passenger liners, Milford Haven has one of the deepest natural harbours in the world. The regenerated waterfront and marina offers a fantastic collection of cafes, restaurants, bars and 'knick knack' shops. The waterfront is an ideal place to sit down, relax and unwind with a coffee as you watch the world (and boats) go by.

OAKWOOD THEME PARK
CANASTON BRIDGE,
SA67 8DE
///FIGHTS.UNIONISTS.
BULLDOZER

Wales' biggest theme park! A perfect day out to mix up your road trip itinerary, I mean surely you're sick of all them incredible beaches by now? Oakwood has a number of thrill and family rides plus seasonal events to look out for. It's best to buy tickets in advance for the best prices.

PEMBROKE CASTLE
PEMBROKE,
SA71 4LA
///WORKSHOP.CRYPT.
SUBJECT

A mighty medieval castle situated in the centre of Pembroke! Most of the structure that stands today was constructed in the 12th century and is one of the most complete and best preserved castles in Wales. Adult tickets are £8.50 / Kids & Seniors are £6.00 and can be purchased upon arrival to the castle. There are a number free guided tours running throughout the day and the castle is completely dog friendly!

144

FRESHWATER WEST

ST GOVANS CHAPEL

FRESHWATER WEST
HAVERFORDWEST,
SA71 5AH
///ROBE.RETRACED.PAGES

Another must visit Pembrokeshire beach, if you're a Harry Potter fan you will love it! If you didn't guess, there are quite a few impeccable beaches to add to your road trip in this area. Freshwater West is the best place for surfing in Pembrokeshire and therefore the best place to watch surfing if you don't fancy giving it a go yourself. I really enjoyed getting on the bodyboard on my last visit here (although I certainly need some practice). This wild & sandy paradise has limited free parking along the sand dunes. Harry Potter fans will be able to see Dobby's grave which was featured in the film Harry Potter and the Deathly Hallows. Dogs are allowed all year (if you're not a fan of dogs this place is bloody huge so don't worry about it).

ELEGUG STACKS, GREEN BRIDGE & CAULDRON
PEMBROKE,
SA71 5HT
///OWNS.FERRYING.JEEP

Located just 6 miles from Freshwater West are the interesting 'Green Bridge, Elegug Stacks & The Cauldron' coastal geological features. The Green Bridge is a naturally formed arch carved out of the cliffside and quite a sight to behold. The Elegug Sea Stacks and The Cauldron are equally unique and certainly worth a look at. Just please take care along the cliffside, The 'Stack Rocks' car park here is free but access is sometimes restricted due to MOD Live Firing exercises at the nearby firing range. Also double check you have the correct place programmed into Google Maps or your Sat Nav, many people (including myself) end up elsewhere. I actually ended up at St Govans Chapel which is a 20 minute drive away.

ST GOVANS CHAPEL
ST. GOVAN'S HEAD,
BOSHERSTON,
SA71 5DR
///NAVIGATE.MADNESS.
APPROVALS

I accidentally stumbled across this place and I'm glad I did! St Govans is a tiny chapel consisting of two chambers built into the side of a limestone cliff. Parts of it were believed to date back to the 6th century and one legend suggests that St Govan is buried underneath it. The chapel is open year round, is completely free and is accessible from the clifftop by climbing down a set of 52 steps. Count the steps up and down again, legend has it that the numbers are never the same! How peculiar? When we visited in the summer, there was an ice cream van parked above St Govans. Be warned though, it wasn't a whipped ice cream, merely a tub of Asda frozen scooped into a cone.

 @ROBBIEROAMS

BARAFUNDLE BAY BEACH
SA71 5LS
///UNDERTOOK.DART.
LESSENING

This beach is unbelievable, wow! One of, if not the best beach in Pembrokeshire, Barafundle is a beautiful sandy bay backed by dunes and pine trees. It has been voted many times as one of the best beaches in the UK and when you make the half mile walk from Stackpole Quay car park over the cliffs to Barafundle, you'll see why! The walk involves a small set of steep steps from the car park and again once you reach the beach but the part in between is easy and will provide spectacular views out to sea. Barafundle is dog friendly year round, has pristine clear blue waters and is the perfect place for a beach day or a wild winter walk. I was like a kid at Christmas when I first went here!

FRESHWATER EAST
TREWENT HILL,
PEMBROKE,
SA71 5LY
///QUOTE.ZOOS.CLOUDS

Almost a mirror image of the beautiful 'Freshwater West' beach, this golden sandy heaven features a stream running through the middle and has parking available nearby. Freshwater East is generally safe for swimming (although not manned by a lifeguard) and is popular with families and dog owners. There are toilets, a café and shop nearby.

SKRINKLE HAVEN BEACH & CHURCH DOOR COVE
MANORBIER,
SA70 7SH
///FIGHTS.UNIONISTS.
BULLDOZER

Another area of geological interest and a magnificent photo opportunity, Skrinkle Haven Beach is a unique hard to access spot that can be found right next to Church Door cove. To get to the beach you will need to make your way down some steep steps (to Church Door Cove) which may be challenging for some visitors. Skrinkle Haven can then be accessed by walking around the limestone ridge (although this is only possible at low tide). Please take care on the cliff edge and be aware of the tides. As an alternative, there is also a picturesque picnic site at the top of the pathway that allows you to take in the views over the bay. This spot is magnificent for photos. Church Door Cove features an unusual cliff arch that looks like a 'Church Door' funnily enough. There's a carpark at the nearby YHA Manorbier.

TOP TIP

IF YOU'RE PHYSICALLY ABLE, YOU REALLY CANNOT MISS BARAFUNDLE BAY BEACH!

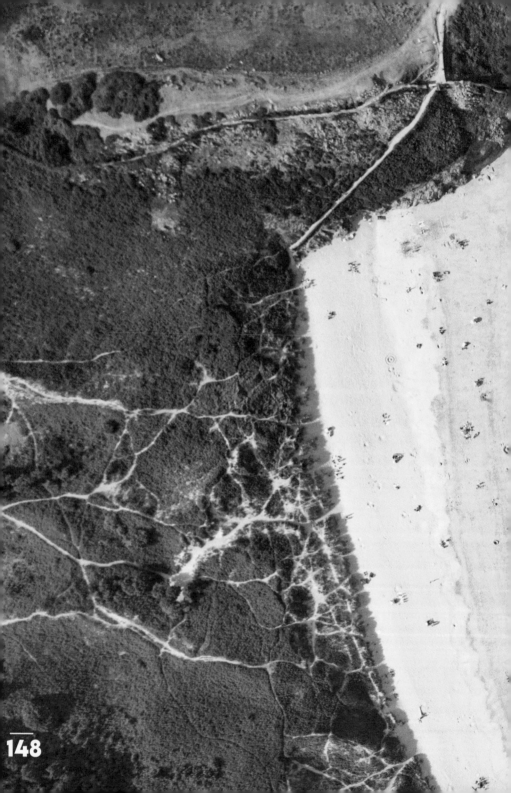

BARAFUNDLE BAY

CALDEY ISLAND
TENBY,
SA70 7UJ
///RACING.SHELVING.LISTS

Situated around 1 mile from the coast of Tenby lies Caldey Island, home to the Cistercian monks. With a recorded history going back over 1,500 years, it is one of the holy islands of Britain. The Island has a number of attractions including The Monastery and Abbey, a chocolate factory and a number of relaxing walks where you can see great beaches, scenic lighthouses and picturesque woodland. Boats to Caldey run from April to October and tickets are obtained from the Caldey Island Kiosk at the top of Tenby Harbour. All tickets are return and are priced at £15 for Adults and £9 for Children. The island is closed on Sunday.

TENBY
SA70 8AG
///GHOST.GROSS.TOKEN

One of Wales' most picturesque and iconic sea side towns, there is a lot to love about Tenby! Surrounded by an historic medieval wall, Tenby has a maze of narrow streets packed with bars, restaurants and quirky shops. It has three terrific sandy beaches which provide picture perfect views of Tenby Castle and Palmerston Fort on St Catherine's Island (which is accessible during low tide). The Harbour and Lifeboat Station are certainly worth checking out and if you have kids with you, the nearby Dinosaur Park may get you into the good books! Tenby is an essential location for any road trip that crosses South Wales, what a charming and wonderful place. I seriously can't wait to go back! The North Beach Car Park is large and is only a 5 minute walk into the town centre if you're struggling - the postcode shown on the left will take you straight there just keep an eye out for the 'North Beach Car Park' signs.

SAUNDERSFOOT BEACH
SAUNDERSFOOT,
SA69 9HE
///SLIDES.COMEDIANS.
THINKERS

Just a few miles north of Tenby is Saundersfoot which offers a gently sloping golden sandy beach with easily accessible parking. It may also be less busy than the nearby Tenby beaches which do receive a lot of people on a warm summer's day. Dogs aren't allowed unfortunately.

TOP TIP

TRY ONE OF THE DELICIOUS PASTY SHOPS IN TENBY, SOME REAL UNIQUE FLAVOURS!

TENBY

WHERE TO STAY...

CAMPING, MOTORHOMES AND CARAVANS

LLEITHYR FARM HOLIDAY PARK
WHITESANDS BAY, ST DAVIDS, SA62 6PR | 01437 720245

An excellent touring and camping facilities, a fantastic site shop and bakery, a children's play area and animal farm walk. Located just a couple of miles from St Davids in Pembrokeshire, stay at Lleithyr Farm is camping and touring at its very best. Me & Jas stayed here during the heatwave of 2022 and loved it! We were able to walk the dogs through the animal walk which they seemed to really enjoy.

FACILITIES...
ELECTRIC HOOK UP
TOILETS
SHOWERS
DOG FRIENDLY
WASTE DISPOSAL
ON SITE SHOP
ANIMAL WALK

PENALLY COURT FARM
PENALLY, TENBY, SA70 7PR | 01834 845109

Penally Court is a small and friendly family run holiday park within minutes of Tenby. The campsite captures all that is best in Pembrokeshire holidays – set in idyllic and tranquil location just inland from the coast with spectacular views over Tenby South Beach.

FACILITIES...
ELECTRIC HOOK UP
TOILETS
SHOWERS
DOG FRIENDLY
WASTE DISPOSAL

HOTELS, BNB'S AND ACCOMMODATION

TWR Y FELIN HOTEL | ££-£££
FFORDD CAERFAI, ST. DAVIDS, SA62 6QT | 01437 725555

A former windmill and Wales' first contemporary art hotel located in St Davids. This hotel is a little more expensive but has very high ratings and you generally get what you pay for.

WOLFSCASTLE COUNTRY HOTEL | ££-£££
WOLF'S CASTLE, HAVERFORDWEST, SA62 5LZ | 01437 741225

Winner of 'Welsh Romantic Hotel' of the year! Providing an ideal mix of value, comfort and convenience, it offers a charming setting and it even has an on-site spa.

BEAVERS RETREAT GLAMPING | ££-£££
THE RIDGEWAY, TENBY, SA70 8LQ | 01834 871545

A mix of luxurious geodomes and bell tents with wood burners and hot tubs. Located on the outskirts of Tenby, this is a unique glamping experience perfect for all the family.

TOP TIP

LLEITHYR FARM HOLIDAY PARK IS A TOP CAMPSITE WITH OR WITHOUT KIDS!

SKRINKLE HAVEN

WHERE TO EAT & DRINK

THE REALLY WILD EMPORIUM | SEAFOOD & VEGAN OPTIONS
24 HIGH STREET, ST. DAVIDS, SA62 6SD

THE PEMBROKE YEOMAN | GREAT FOOD & LIVE MUSIC PUB
11 HILL STREET, HAVERFORDWEST, SA61 1QQ

WAVECREST CAFE | FANTASTIC LUNCH AND LIGHT BITES
WEST ANGLE BAY, PEMBROKE, SA71 5BE

FUCHSIA | TEA, COFFEE, BREAKFASTS
UPPER FROG STREET, TENBY, SA68 0TB

A DILEMMA ON THE HOTTEST DAY IN HISTORY!

During our recent Welsh Coast 400 road trip (which you can watch on my Youtube channel), the UK was experiencing an unprecedented heatwave which resulted in temperatures
of 40 degrees celsius! Now you're probably thinking, I'd love to be on a road trip near the
beach during a heatwave, however, we had two dogs to worry about keeping cool. For the
most part, the constant sea breeze and cold sea water was doing a great job at keeping
Archie and Gem happy. During the drive between locations, the aircon in the van was a
life saver (I had it re-gassed before the trip). On our drive to Tenby, Jas received a phone
call notifying her of a last minute hospital appointment and if she wasn't able to attend,
the next appointment would be 3 months away. This caused a big dilemma! Do we drive
4 hours home to get to the appointment and end the trip early? Do we just carry on the
trip and knock back the hospital? In the end we decided to drive 4 hours there, get to the
appointment and drive 4 hours back to Tenby. This may sound like madness, and it was, but,
the dogs were as cool as cucumber lapping up the aircon whilst outside was a blistering 41
degrees! It was a long old day but we were happy to return to Tenby and finish off the trip.

CARMARTHENSHIRE, THE GOWER & SWANSEA

RHOSSILI BAY

CARMARTHENSHIRE, THE GOWER & SWANSEA

KIDWELLY CASTLE

THE WILD & EPIC SOUTH COAST!

Huge ancient castles, vast areas of outstanding natural beauty and the birthplace of legendary Welsh poet, Dylan Thomas, this part of South Wales had endless charm everywhere you turn. The Gower is one of my favourite parts of Wales, it truly is a tremendous peninsula with some of the UK's best beaches.

MUST SEES...

KIDWELLY CASTLE

NATIONAL BOTANIC GARDEN OF WALES

THE GOWER PENINSULA

THE MUMBLES

THINGS TO SEE AND DO...

KIDWELLY CASTLE / CASTELL CYDWELI
CASTLE RD,
KIDWELLY,
SA17 5BQ
///STUN.QUALIFIED.PLANT

First constructed in the early 12th century, Kidwelly is a superb medieval fortress located in Carmarthenshire overlooking the River Gwendraeth. It's a mighty and imposing monument of Norman power. The origin of the surname traces back to when it was spelled Cygweli which means "swan." Film nerds will easily recognise the castle from the opening scene of Monty Python and the Holy Grail! Tickets are fairly priced at £6.50 for Adults / £4.60 for Juniors (5-17) and £6.00 for Seniors (65+).

@ROBBIEROAMS

CEFN SIDAN BEACH & PEMBREY COUNTRY PARK

PEMBREY,
BURRY PORT,
SA16 0EJ
///CARELESS.CONTRACTING.
ACTIVATES

Wales' first Blue Flag beach and arguably its longest at just over 8 miles long. Located 4 miles South of Kidwelly, Cefn Sidan is a place many people haven't ever heard of and with so much beach to go around, you can certainly enjoy some peace and quiet here. The beach is part of the Pembrey Country Park which boasts 500 acres of park and woodland with multiple trails and activities such as a ski slope and toboggan.

THE NATIONAL BOTANIC GARDEN OF WALES

MIDDLETON HALL,
LLANARTHNE,
SA32 8HN
///PRONOUNS.LEGEND.
PACKAGES

Described as 'an enchanting mosaic of flower-rich meadows, evocative woodlands, waterfalls and cascades' – The National Botanic Garden of Wale s is a fabulous location to bring you closer to nature. Having received a lot of restoration over the last 5 years, the garden is perfect for all ages and also features The British Bird of Prey Centre who run bird flying displays daily. Adult tickets are £13.75 with deals available for families for example, 2 Adults & 2, 3 or 4 Children for £39.75.

THE GOWER PENINSULA

SA3 1HX
///TANGENT.AVOIDING.
SKIDDING

I'd heard about The Gower but hadn't fully researched it, so upon my first drive to Rhossili Bay my mind was actually blown! It was the first place in the UK to be a designated Area of Outstanding Natural Beauty and when you visit you'll see the reasons why. The Gower is a vast and varied environment made up of wild moors, dramatic limestone cliffs and epic never ending beaches. At times, driving through the open moors you'll feel like you're in the wilderness as you pass wild horses and grazing cattle (please be careful and give them a wide berth). At this point in the book, you may be sick of me talking about beaches, but hear me out, some of these Gower beaches are quite honestly the best I've seen in the UK and comparable with beaches across the world!

THE GOWER MINI ROAD TRIP

SEE THE BEST OF THE GOWER IN THIS EPIC MINI ROAD TRIP TAKING 1 DAY OR SPREAD IT OUT OVER A WEEKEND. SCAN THE QR CODE ON THE RIGHT FOR DIRECTIONS ON GOOGLE MAPS.

THE MUMBLES

RHOSSILI BAY
GOWER,
SA3 1JD
///PALETTES.NARRATES.
BADLY

THIS PLACE IS AMAZING! Described as *'The supermodel of British beaches'* by The Independent and winner of many number one beach awards, Rhossili Bay is truly one of a kind. The Worms Head Car Park provides an almost *'drone like'* view of this spectacular beach and is highly recommended to allow you to take in the 3 miles of sheer beauty. Access to the beach from here is tricky at best with very steep steps taking you down the cliffside and eventually down to the beach. We didn't fancy that option, so instead, we got back on the road and headed to the Hill End Camping Park which has a car park right next to the beach and costs £5 for the day. Just be warned, the drive from Worms Head to Hill End is around 30 minutes but it's completely worth it for easy access to the beach. As Rhossili is so bloody big, you'll be miles away from the nearest beach-goer and good news if you have your four legged friends with you as The Times nominated Rhossili as *'The UK's No.1 dog-friendly beach'*. If I could choose just one beach in the whole of Wales to visit, I think it would be this one!

OXWICH BAY
SA3 1LS
///SUFFICE.REEF.COMPLY

Another pristine, vast, golden stretch of sand which is gently sloping making it ideal for taking a dip. The car park is very conveniently located (almost on the beach) and dogs are welcome year round. Most of the facilities including the beach café & beach house restaurant are near to the carpark and the village of Oxwich. The further you walk from the carpark towards Tor Bay to the east, the quieter and more relaxing this wonderful location becomes.

THREE CLIFFS BAY
SA3 2HB
///TROPIC.HOWEVER.GROUP

A landscape photographers dream! Three Cliffs Bay Beach is a super scenic sandy beach featuring three limestone cliffs making for a dramatic backdrop. With a stream running through the centre of the bay and panoramic views from the cliffs, it's not difficult to see why it's one of the most photographed areas in South Wales. Parking & toilets are located around 400m away at the Three Cliffs Bay Holiday Park and dogs are allowed all year. It's not too far from Oxwich Bay & Tor Bay so think about combining these locations in the same day.

CASWELL BAY & LANGLAND BAY
SWANSEA,
SA3 3BR
///CONFIDENT.PRESSES.
THRONES

Caswell Bay is a very accessible Blue Flag Beach popular with families & surfers. With toilets, external showers and a surfside café, Caswell Bay is an ideal location for a beach day. Langland Bay is just 1.2 miles along the coastal clifftop path (or 5 minutes on the road) from Caswell Bay and is yet another fine beach with excellent facilities in this marvelous part of South Wales! Dogs aren't permitted at either beach from May-September.

THE MUMBLES
SA3 4EE
///POETRY.FINER.NOTED

Depending on which direction you're heading, The Mumbles marks the start / end of The Gower Peninsula and is a well-loved area of Swansea! One of Dylan Thomas' former stomping grounds and with much to see and do, The Mumbles has a little bit of something for everyone. It's fantastic for foodies, perfect for shopping and even has an iconic Victorian Pier and 12th century castle. It's well known as the birth place of Catherine Zeta Jones and the infamous 'Mumbles Mile' with its many pubs!

SWANSEA
SA1 3RD
///VOTED.TRIALS.TOXIC

Wales' second-largest city and birthplace of legendary Welsh poet - Dylan Thomas! Swansea is a university city packed with buzzing bars and lively restaurants contrasted with art galleries, historical locations and museums. By day you can explore places such as the National Waterfront Museum, Swansea Castle and the Dylan Thomas Centre. By night get your glad rags on and visit the Swansea Grand Theatre & Wind Street (home to many restaurants and bars including 'No Sign' a previous favorite of Dylan Thomas).

SWANSEA BEACH
SA3 2HB
///LOWER.WISER.SECURE

Often overlooked by visitors to The Gower's outstanding beaches, Swansea Bay Beach is conveniently located just minutes from the heart of the city centre and is clean, sandy and huge! I have fond memories of visiting this beach during a university taster weekend with my sixth form college many years ago. We lit a huge fire, drank a lot of beer and watched the sunset before frantically running back to our uni dorms before our curfew! Good times and a cracking location indeed.

CARMARTHENSHIRE, THE GOWER & SWANSEA

SOUTH WALES

 ROBBIEROAMS.COM

WHERE TO STAY...

CAMPING, MOTORHOMES AND CARAVANS ⛺

HILLEND CARAVAN & CAMPING PARK
LLANGENNITH, HILLEND, SA3 1JD | 01792 386204

Perfectly located next to Rhosilli Bay on The Gower Peninsula! This highly rated campsite has an onsite cafe and bar open April-October and fantastic facilities. The main reason I've featured this campsite is that it offers the most accessible way on to the mind blowing Rhossili Bay Beach! A simple 100-200 yard walk through the dunes will lead you onto this award winning beach.

FACILITIES...
ELECTRIC HOOK UP
TOILETS
SHOWERS
WASTE DISPOSAL
ON SITE BAR
NO DOGS ALLOWED

THREE CLIFFS BAY HOLIDAY PARK
N HILLS LN, PENMAEN, SA3 2HB | 01792 371218

A Five Star holiday park offering luxury Glamping, Camping and Touring pitches. Just a short walk from the infamous Three Cliffs Bay on The Gower Peninsula. This dog friendly site is one of the highest rated campsites in the whole of Wales!

FACILITIES...
ELECTRIC HOOK UP
TOILETS
SHOWERS
SHOP
DOG FRIENDLY
WASTE DISPOSAL

HOTELS, BNB'S AND ACCOMMODATION

LLANERCHINDDA FARMHOUSE | ££-£££
CYNGHORDY, LLANDOVERY, SA20 0NB | 01550 750274

A wonderful countryside guesthouse & self catering cottages with views of the Cynghordy viaduct and mountains beyond. Also offering a number of outdoor activities.

KING ARTHUR HOTEL | ££-£££
HIGHER GREEN, REYNOLDSTON, GOWER, SA3 1AD | 01792 390775

Recently named as The Times 'Top cosy pub in the UK', the King Arthur's charming ambience is hard to beat. Comfortable and tastefully furnished rooms.

THE GRAND HOTEL SWANSEA | ££-£££
IVEY PL, SWANSEA, SA1 1NX | 01792 645898

A landmark hotel since the 1930's, largely due to its ideal location and unique design. Reasonably priced rooms and rated as 'Very Good' on booking.com

TOP TIP

STOP FOR FOOD AT THE KINGS HEAD INN LOCATED NEAR RHOSSILI BAY! DELICIOUS.

SWANSEA

WHERE TO EAT & DRINK

THE WARREN | WELSH & BRITISH CLASSICS
11 MANSEL STREET, CARMARTHEN, SA31 1PX

KINGS HEAD INN | FABULOUS HEARTY MEALS
CLOS ST CENYDD, LLANGENNITH, SA3 1HX

GOWER SEAFOOD HUT | FRESH GRAB AND GO SEAFOOD
PROMENADE TERRACE, THE SLIP, MUMBLES, SWANSEA, SA3 4DS

TRUFFLE RESTAURANT | THE BEST IN SWANSEA
1A KING EDWARDS ROAD, SWANSEA, SA1 4LH

PROBABLY THE BEST BEACH IN THE UK...

If Carlsberg made British beaches, then Rhossili bay would probably be the best (by my standards). On our recent Welsh Coast 400 trip, we made our way down to the Gower Peninsula for the first time. Driving across the vast moorland felt as though we had entered the wilderness. The sun was shining, Wales was on the back of a record breaking heatwave and we were heading in the direction of the nearest beach which just so happened to be Rhossili bay. We initially drove to the Worms Head car park which gives you an amazing 'drone like' view across the bay. Unfortunately, access from here isn't easy and we were told off by a grumpy old man for leaving our engine running whilst we plotted our next move (the aircon was running for the dogs so he could get stuffed). We decided to head to the Hill End car park which placed us right onto the middle section of the beach. Me, Jas & the two dogs made our way through the dunes and onto this pristine slice of beach heaven. We had at least half a mile of beach to ourselves! The sea was mild, there were a few decent waves I could tackle with my body board and I couldn't quite believe that I was in the UK. A genuinely remarkable beach, probably my favourite in the UK.

CARDIFF

PORTHCAWL LIGHTHOUSE

CARDIFF

CARDIFF

THE BUZZING CAPITAL OF WALES!

Cardiff is a compact, friendly capital city ready to welcome everyone and anyone! With pop-up dining, intimate gigs and global sporting events it all seems to be going on. It has a spectacular castle, and a 76,000 seater stadium right in the heart of the city. The surrounding areas are also worth visiting!

MUST SEES...

PORTHCAWL

BARRY ISLAND

CARDIFF CASTLE

CARDIFF MARKET

CARDIFF BAY

CHIPPY LANE

THINGS TO SEE AND DO...

PORTHCAWL TO LLANTWIT MAJOR

PORTHCAWL,
CF36 3XA
///FORKLIFT.DESCRIBES.
WISER

This area of South Wales is often overlooked but has plenty to offer! First of all, Porthcawl Rest Bay has miles of fine golden sand and is a hotspot for water sports with its new state-of-the-art water sports centre. It has blue flag status and plenty of facilities including toilets, café, accessible parking and lifeguards during the summer. Porthcawl town centre has a number of attractions including a funfair, promenade and the picturesque Porthcawl Lighthouse which is a great place to watch huge waves crash in on a windy day. Newton Beach located just to the east of...

Porthcawl is alternate beach option which allows dogs (unlike Rest Bay). Ogmore By Sea Beach is a good 20 minute drive south of Porthcawl and is perfect for rockpooling, fossil hunting and cave exploring. The scenic Dunraven Bay is just a 10 minute drive south of Ogmore and doesn't get as busy as other beaches in the area. Continuing south in the Direction of LLantwit Major is the historic Nash Point Lighthouse. This lighthouse was constructed in 1832 following 'The Frolic' steam vessel tragedy which claimed 78 lives. Nash Point makes for a superb photo and is a terrific place to stretch the legs and take a café break at after a long drive. Finally, the Llantwit Major Beach is popular with dog walkers and rockpool hunters and although it isn't sandy, offers some superb photo opportunities if that's your thing.

BARRY ISLAND
BARRY,
CF62 5TQ
///RUBBLE.EDGES.WINKS

A vibrant seaside resort which was the backdrop of many iconic scenes in BBC's award winning *'Gavin & Stacey',* tidy! Now don't get me wrong, Barry Island isn't for everyone, but, it offers some light-hearted fun with its arcades, pleasure park and fish and chip shops. If you're a Gavin & Stacey fan like me, you can do a mini tour of some of the key locations including Nessa's Slots, Marco's Café and of course Gwen & Stacey's house located on Trinity Street. We visited all of these spots and I even shouted *'what's occurring?'* to the owner of Gwen & Stacey's house which was greeted with complete silence (unbelievably cringey), but, you only live once and all that. Barry is situated about 20 minutes from nearby Penarth and 30 minutes from Cardiff so it makes for an easy stop off if you're heading in that direction.

PENARTH
CF64 2AH
///ASHES.HOST.JOKE

A charming seaside town with a Victorian Pier, delightful esplanade and contemporary marina. There are some lovely parks located in between the coast and the town centre with Cosmeston Lakes Country Park and Medieval Village the top attraction boasting over 100 hectares of land and water filled with all kinds of wildlife. The country park is dog friendly and ideal for a morning or afternoon walk.

CARDIFF CITY

CF10 3RB

///HEARS.CROWDS.GOES

The capital and largest city in Wales! Cardiff seems to tick all boxes from castles to culture and watersports to pubs! Within 1 mile of the city centre, Cardiff has pretty much everything you can think of. But where to begin? Cardiff Castle will provide panoramic views over the city and with tickets priced at £13.50 for Adults and £9.50 for Children, is a solid place to start. The nearby National Museum of Wales could be the next stop to help you get a better understanding on the evolution of Wales. If you time your trip right, you'll be able to watch a fierce game of rugby or perhaps even a boxing match at the principality stadium. St Mary's street has a number of Edwardian and Victorian shopping arcades packed with an array of cafes and independent shops. The entrance to Cardiff Market is also on St Mary's street and is home to a number of sellers from fishmongers to bakeries (don't forget to grab a Welsh Cake). A five minute train journey from Queen Street station is Cardiff Bay. This former industrial site has been developed over the last 30 years and is a popular spot for tourists and locals. There's lots of great restaurants and cafes overlooking Cardiff Bay at Mermaid Quay where you can also take a boat ride out into the bay for a different view of Cardiff. The spectacular Wales Millennium Centre is located in Cardiff Bay and attracts performers from all over the world. Other places of note include Castell Coch, St Fagans National Musuem, Roath Park & Bute Park. A night out in Cardiff has just about everything you could wish for! Live music, nightclubs, quirky bars and a buzzing atmosphere. Clwb Ifor Bach is the place to be for live music. For a traditional pub head to City Arms or Pen and Wig. End your night at the iconic Caroline Street known as 'chippy lane' – a tradition followed by many locals. I highly rate this place after a few jars that's for sure!

TOP TIP

CARDIFF IS PACKED IF WALES ARE PLAYING AT THE PRINCIPALITY STADIUM, THERE'S A GREAT ATMOSHPHERE AND BARS ARE BUSY. ALTHOUGH, YOU MAY WISH TO AVOID THIS.

CARDIFF CASTLE

WHERE TO STAY...

CAMPING, MOTORHOMES AND CARAVANS

BRODAWEL CAMPING AND CARAVAN PARK
MOOR LN, PORTHCAWL, CF36 3EJ | 01656 783231

A popular family run caravan and camping park on the outskirts of Nottage, Porthcawl with its collection of fine sandy beaches and many coves and fertile rock pools. With excellent touring and camping facilities, a fantastic site shop and a children's play area, a stay at Brodawel offers everything you need for a wonderful road trip stop off! The closest touring and camping park to Rest Bay.

FACILITIES...
ELECTRIC HOOK UP
TOILETS
SHOWERS
DOG FRIENDLY
WASTE DISPOSAL
ON SITE SHOP
ANIMAL WALK

CARDIFF CARAVAN AND CAMPING PARK
FIELDS PARK RD, CARDIFF, CF11 9XR | 029 2039 8362

Cardiff Caravan Park is situated in beautiful parkland close to the heart of the city, and makes an ideal base from which to explore the many and varied attractions in and around Cardiff. There aren't any better locations so close to the city centre!

FACILITIES...
ELECTRIC HOOK UP
TOILETS
SHOWERS
DOG FRIENDLY
WASTE DISPOSAL

HOTELS, BNB'S AND ACCOMMODATION

OLIVIA HOUSE | ££-£££
44 ESPLANADE AVENUE, PORTHCAWL, CF36 3YU | 07968 841992

Offering exclusive and stylish accommodation in a unique recently refurbished Edwardian townhouse, just 50 metres from the picturesque Porthcawl promenade.

THE COAL EXCHANGE HOTEL CARDIFF | ££-£££
4-5 MOUNT STUART SQUARE, CARDIFF, CF10 5FQ | 029 2199 1904

A 3* luxury hotel in Cardiff Bay steeped in history and the perfect location from which you can explore all that Cardiff has to offer.

VOCO ST. DAVID'S CARDIFF | ££-£££
HAVANNAH STREET, CARDIFF, CF10 5SD | 029 2045 4045

A highly acclaimed, landmark luxury five star hotel on Cardiff Bay. Host to iconic architecture, the award winning Spa at St. David's and destination dining.

TOP TIP

CARDIFF HOTELS ARE FAR CHEAPER IF THERE ISN'T AN EVENT AT THE STADIUM.

BARRY ISLAND

WHERE TO EAT & DRINK

DOCKSIDE BAR AND GRILL | GREAT ALL ROUNDER
2-4 DOCK STREET, PORTHCAWL, CF36 3BL

BUSY TEAPOT | FANTASTIC BREAKFASTS & LUNCH
27 GLEBE STREET, PENARTH, CF64 1EE

FRESH THE BAGUETTE BAR | THE BEST SANDWICH IN CARDIFF
32 ROYAL ARCADE MORGAN QUARTER, CARDIFF, CF10 1AE

VIVO AMIGO CARDIFF | MEXICAN MEETS INDIAN
138 WHITCHURCH ROAD, CARDIFF, CF14 3LZ

A BARMY WEEKEND IN CARDIFF!

I recently spent a weekend in Cardiff with a group of friends we met on a tour in Bolivia during our South America trip early in 2022. We decided to have a reunion in Cardiff as most of the group wanted to watch the singer Paulo Nutini and the dates seemed to align perfectly. The city was absolutely buzzing! Wales were playing at the Principality Stadium on the Saturday so the bars and restaurants were packed all weekend. The Friday evening we attended the Paulo Nutini gig (which was awful I might add) and then headed to check out some of the bars and pubs. The nightlife in Cardiff is bloody brilliant. It's condensed into such a small area meaning you don't have to spend half your night walking for miles. We ended up in a couple of charming boozers and then went to a place where you could hire your own private karaoke booth. Our night ended at the famous chippy lane where we all devoured some delicious greasy fast food. On the Saturday we headed back into the city where we did an escape room, checked out the castle, explored some of the beautiful victorian style shopping arcades and went for dinner at an Indian street food restaurant. A memorable and hilarious weekend in such a fantastic city with so much to see and do!

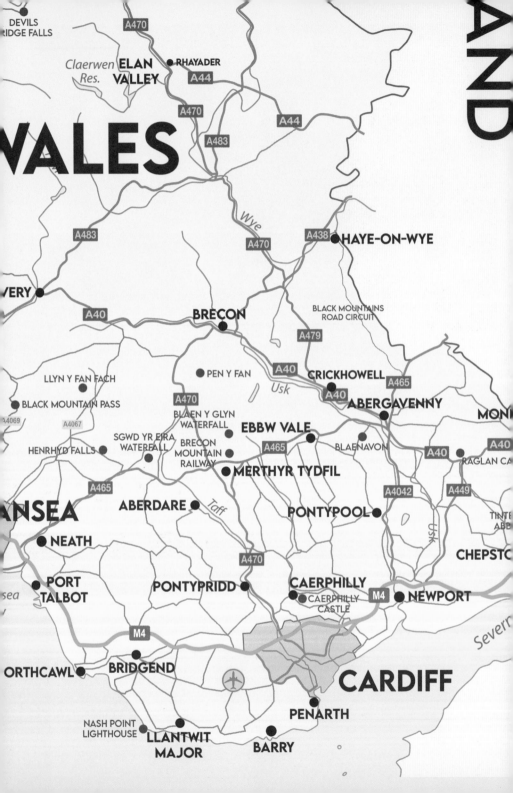

BRECON BEACONS & THE SOUTH EAST

· ·

BRECON BEACONS & THE SOUTH EAST

TINTERN ABBEY

NATURAL BEAUTY AT ITS FINEST...

The Brecon Beacons and South East of Wales offer a mix of outstanding natural beauty and lively market towns filled with culture and history. Explore some of the iconic mountain passes, try some adrenaline fuelled outdoor activities and mooch around the charming towns and villages. A beatiful part of the world.

MUST SEES...

CAERPHILLY CASTLE
CRICKHOWELL
GOSPEL PASS
PEN Y FAN
HAYE-ON-WYE
HENRHYD FALLS

THINGS TO SEE AND DO...

CAERPHILLY CASTLE

CASTLE ST,
CAERPHILLY,
CF83 1JD
///GRACE.NASAL.NAILS

Described as the 'mightiest' medieval castle in Wales! Caerphilly Castle was constructed by Gilbert de Clare in the 13th century as part of his campaign to maintain control of Glamorgan. It's Wales' largest castle and offers an awe inspiring visit for people of all ages. Tickets are £10.10 for Adults, £7.10 for Children and £9.50 for Seniors. Dogs are welcome and can access everywhere on the ground floor of the castle. Will you visit the largest castle in Wales?

 @ROBBIEROAMS

TINTERN ABBEY
TINTERN,
NP16 6SE
///BELONGING.RANT.SHRUB

First founded in 1131 by Cistercian Monks, Tintern Abbey is a national icon standing on the banks of the River Wye. Located between Chepstow and Monmouth, Tintern Abbey has a fascinating history to match its picturesque beauty. During the romantic period it was visited by poets and painters such as Wordsworth and Turner. It is still one of Wales most photographed locations and entry costs £8.30 Adults / £5.80 Children / £7.70 Seniors.

RAGLAN CASTLE
CASTLE RD,
RAGLAN,
NP15 2BT
///SPLIT.LOAF.BLURS

Another fine example of a medieval Welsh castle claimed to be the 'grandest' castle built by a Welshmen. Set in glorious countryside, Raglan Castle was designed to impress as much as to intimidate. This area of Wales is blessed with many impressive castles and Raglan is right up there. Dogs are welcome and entry costs £8.30 Adults / £5.80 Children / £7.70 Seniors.

BLAENAVON
PONTYPOOL,
NP4 9AS
///HAZELNUTS.SELECT.
UNAFRAID

Blaenavon is a world heritage site with a number of must see attractions such as Big Pit National Coal Museum, Blaenavon Ironworks, the World Heritage Centre and Blaenavon Heritage Railway which are all just a few minutes' drive or walk from each other. This historic industrial town set on the outskirts of the Brecon Beacons National Park rapidly grew after the ironworks were opened by the West Midlands industrialist, Thomas Hill, in 1788.

CRICKHOWELL
HIGH ST,
CRICKHOWELL,
NP8 1BE
///MILKMAN.CHAIRS.
KNOWLEDGE

This picturesque town nestling in the wonderful Usk Valley is a popular location to use as a base for exploring the nearby hills and mountains. I would definitely recommend stopping to walk across Crickhowell's famous 18th century bridge which makes for a lovely photo opportunity. The Monmouthshire & Brecon canal is just 1 mile from Crickhowell and hiring an electric day boat, canoe or paddleboard is a peaceful way to spend an afternoon. If you fancy a bit of that, Beacon Park Boats in Llangattock is the place to go. It's also home to Crickhowell Castle, also known as Alisby's castle, a conspicuous feature of the small market town and occupies a vantage point with commanding views along the Usk valley.

PEN Y FAN

BRECON MOUNTAIN RAILWAY
PONTSTICILL RD, PANT, CF48 2DD
///MEALS.FORUM.WEDS

A unique and enjoyable way to take in the fantastic views of the Brecon Beacons. The Brecon Mountain Railway goes through Pontsticill and along the full length of the Taf Fechan Reservior before climbing to Torpantau high in the Brecon Beacons and the summit of the original line. On the way back down there's a handy 25-30 minute stop at the museum and café. Dogs are welcome and bare in mind the railway is only open between April-October. At the time of writing there were roadworks in and around the area so please allow extra time to arrive.

BLACK MOUNTAINS ROAD CIRCUIT
ABERGAVENNY, HR3 5RJ
///HELPFUL.FORMATION.GADGETS

This 49 mile circular route offers some of the most scenic and jaw dropping landscapes in the whole of Wales. I accidentally drove over the Gospel Pass (part of this circuit) and was completely in awe of the views! It's funny how taking a wrong turn can turn out so well isn't it? Without stopping, this circuit will take you around 2 hours but I'd recommend a whole day so you can stop at Hay-on-Wye, Crickhowell and of course pull over for some epic photos! Now, this route can be taken clockwise or anti-clockwise depending on your next destination, but for arguments sake, let's start in Abergavenny and head anti-clockwise. (If you scan the QR code on the left with your smartphone you can load the route on Google maps). First of all head north on the A465 to Llanvihangel Crucorney. Then it's a right in the direction of Llanthony which will turn into a single track road. You then follow the road right through to Gospel Pass where the views of the mountains and valley below will have you on the edge of your seat. The road descends towards the next destination Haye-on-Wye before heading South West towards Glasbury. After passing by Talgarth you'll head towards Crickhowell before completing the circuit at Abergavenny. If time isn't on your side, this circuit is perfect to experience the beautiful Brecons!

TOP TIP 👍

THE BLACK MOUNTAINS ROAD CIRCUIT IS NOT TO BE MISSED! BREAKTAKING ROUTE!

BLAEN Y GLYN WATERFALLS
TALYBONT-ON-USK,
MERTHYR TYDFIL,
CF48 2UT
///THINKING.HEADLINER.
SECTION

This 1 mile circular trail has a mix of woodland, open hills and breathtaking scenery which passes some impressive waterfalls. There are also several plunge pools if you fancy cooling off on a hot summers day. Start at the Blaen y Glyn Isaf car park, the route is circular so you have the option to head clockwise or anti-clockwise. If you head clockwise, you'll start the walk on gravel path which does head uphill but isn't particularly steep. To reach the main falls continue on the main path through a small wooden gate and be sure not to cross the bridge. You'll need to follow the rocky river bed which can be slippery when wet so please take care.

HAYE-ON-WYE
SA3 2HB
///POWERS.DEBATER.TRUMP

The World's First Book town! Haye-On-Wye is uniquely positioned on the border of Wales and England and has over 20 book shops. It also hosts the annual Hay Festival of Literature & Arts which takes place at the end of May / start of June and welcomes a whopping 80,000 guests each year. If you happen to visit Hay on a nice day, check out the Warren - a beautiful riverside meadow popular with locals for swimming! The Thursday market is a small but vibrant market offering the best in fresh and local produce, artisan delicacies and flea stalls. Overall, a thriving little town.

BLACK MOUNTAIN ACTIVITIES
THE ACTIVITY
CENTRE, THREE
COCKS, BRECON,
LD3 0SD
///CAMP.HARDBACK.BOAST

Black Mountain Adventure (also known as Black Mountain Activities) offer a wide range of pursuits including Clay Pigeon Shooting, Gorge Scrambling and White Water Rafting. Throwing an activity into a road trip can really make it a memorable one. I booked the Clay Pigeon Shooting here a few years back for Jas's birthday and it was bloody brilliant! Jas shot way more clays than me of course. The instructor was great and very professional.

BRECON
LD3 7AP
///GOSH.CAVE.ACED

Brecon is a busy market town nestled at the top of the Brecon Beacons. It's known for the famous Brecon Jazz Festival, its independent shops and cafés, vast history, military connections and of course, the magnificent cathedral. The miles of towpath along the Monmouthshire & Brecon Canal can be explored from Brecon on foot or on bike. The Royal Welsh Regimental Museum tells the fascinating story of four of the British army's most famous regiments.

PEN Y FAN
SA3 2HB
///LOWER.WISER.SECURE

The highest peak in South Wales offers magnif-icent views (on a clear day) that will be more than worth the hike up. The 4 mile circular walk from the Storey Arms Outdoor Centre is the most popular route up and is achievable even for those that aren't in the best shape (it's certainly not anything like the climb up Snowdon). In good weather it's possible for children as young as 6 or 7 to reach the summit. Take care if the weather or visibility isn't great and remember it's much colder and more exposed to stronger winds near to the summit so dress appropriately.

NATIONAL SHOW CAVES CENTRE FOR WALES
ABERCRAF,
SA9 1GJ
///DELUDED.BEARINGS.
FUSSY

Voted Britain's Finest Natural Wonder, and the winner of all major environmental and tourism awards. There are three exceptional caves to experience - Dan-yr-Ogof, Cathedral Cave and Bone Cave. Each cave offers a unique underground adventure. Great options for kids and a coffee shop on site.

SGWD YR EIRA WATERFALL
NEATH,
SA11 5US
///QUIETEST.CLUES.
BROADENS

Translated to English, Sgwd yr Eira means the waterfall of snow! It's one of the most famous waterfalls in the Brecon Beacons and is popular with visitors as there's a path that actually goes behind the 50ft falls. Just bear in mind this isn't possible after heavy rain. Sgwd yr Eira is part of the 'Four Falls Walk' which is a 4.5 mile walk and can be accessed by the car park at Cwm Porth (£4 for the day) which has toilets and other facilities. If you're just looking to head straight to Sgwd yr Eira and avoid the full route, head to the smaller car park a few miles down the road (what-3words provided to the left). There are a few rocky paths and steps so it's probably not suitable for anyone with mobility issues but totally worth it if you are able to do so. The route is convenient-ly sign posted.

HENRHYD FALLS
DOL HENRHYD,
COELBREN,
NEATH,
SA10 9PH
///DELUDED.BEARINGS.
FUSSY

The tallest falls in South Wales. Film fans – did you know Henrhyd falls doubled as the Bat Cave in the Batman film The Dark Knight Rises? Yes the trail is steep and can be wet and muddy, but the falls and surrounding gorge are spectacular. To reach Henryhd falls, you can walk straight to the falls from the National Trust Car park (steep and muddy), or you could do the Henrhyd Falls and Nant Llech walk which is a 3.5-mile hike.

SGWD YR EIRA WATERFALL

LLYN-Y-FAN FACH
SA19 9UN
///FEARED.SLANTING.
SUBMITS

A glacial lake in the Brecon Beacons surrounded by stunning trails – a dream for hikers! The remote western side of the Brecon Beacons is virtually untouched compared to the busier eastern side and arguably has the best walks. The Llyn y Fan Fach Walk which starts at the Llyn y Fan Fach Car park, Llangadog, Llanddeusant SA19 9UN, can be done as a 4km there and back walk or an 8km loop. Start on the gravel road uphill from the car park as it immediately follows the Afon Sawdda river. You'll then have a gradual climb past multiple waterfalls and cascades that will lead to a wonderful reveal of Llyn y Fan Fach. From here you can descend back to the car park or continue around the lake to the west and ascend the ridgeline which offers even better views! You must then follow the path along the north-east keeping the lake down to your left before climbing Picws Du before descending into the 'saddle'. From here you must hook a left down a steep trail which zig zags back and forth. Once at the bottom, take the trail on the left which heads back in the direction of the lake. The riverside path will then lead you back down to the car park where you began.

BLACK MOUNTAIN PASS
NEATH,
SA11 5US
///QUIETEST.CLUES.
BROADENS

If you want to take in the best of the Brecon Beacons without leaving your car, camper or motorbike, this is the ultimate road to drive! Scan the QR code on the left! This 23 mile route begins at the junction with the A474 at the north of Gwaun-Cae-Gurwen, and travels through Lower Brynamman and Brynamman. The route then crosses over the Black Mountain range of the Brecon Beacons and emerges near Felindre near Llangadog. It's often claimed to be 'the best road in Wales' and became popular after it was featured on BBC's Top Gear years ago. Don't get this route confused with the previously mentioned 'Black Mountains Road Circuit' which is located on the east of the Brecon Beacons.

DID YOU KNOW?

THE BLACK MOUNTAIN PASS WAS MADE FAMOUS BY BBC'S TOP GEAR!

LLYN-Y-FAN FACH

WHERE TO STAY...

CAMPING, MOTORHOMES AND CARAVANS

TALYBONT FARM CAMPSITE
MILL LN, TALYBONT-ON-USK, LD3 7YJ | 01874 676674

Talybont Farm site is situated on a working farm in a beautiful setting on the edge of a picturesque village in the heart of the Brecon Beacons. The campsite owner is very welcoming and friendly. The village of Talybont is a few minutes walk from the Campsite where you will find a shop, cafe and 2 pubs and there is a park a few minutes further up the road with a children's play area.

FACILITIES...
ELECTRIC HOOK UP
TOILETS
SHOWERS
DOG FRIENDLY
WASTE DISPOSAL

BRECON BEACONS CAMPING & CARAVAN PARK
HEOL TAWE, ABERCRAF, SA9 1GP | 01639 730284

Voted one of the top 25 caravan parks in Britain by a national newspaper. The peace and quiet of the site, together with its beautiful mountain scenery, allow you to unwind and dream away the day. Open 11 months a year.

FACILITIES...
ELECTRIC HOOK UP
TOILETS
SHOWERS
DOG FRIENDLY
WASTE DISPOSAL

HOTELS, BNB'S AND ACCOMMODATION

PETERSTONE COURT HOTEL | £££
LLANHAMLACH, BRECON, LD3 7YB | 01874 665387

A 5-star hotel that provides a friendly face, honest, fresh local food, comfort and a caring team. This is no clichéd country house the atmosphere is relaxed, and informal.

THE OLD RECTORY COUNTRY HOTEL | ££-£££
LLANGATTOCK, CRICKHOWELL, NP8 1PH | 01873 810373

Set amongst 17 acres of beautiful grounds, including an ancient orchard, the building dates back to the 16th century. Highly rated and fabulously located.

THE COACH HOUSE | ££-£££
12 ORCHARD ST, LLANFAES, BRECON, LD3 8AN | 01874 620043

Bed & breakfast with stylish, comfortable and cosy contemporary townhouse, boutique hotel accommodation. Just a few minutes stroll from Brecon town centre.

GOOD TO KNOW

THE BRECON BEACONS CAMPING & CARAVAN PARK IS LOCATED AT THE NATIONAL SHOW-CAVES CENTRE FOR WALES.

BRECON

WHERE TO EAT & DRINK

NEW INN | DELICIOUS HOMEMADE FOOD
OLD ROAD, BWLCH, BRECON BEACONS NATIONAL PARK, LD3 7RQ

HOP IN BEER & GIN | GREAT BEER, GREAT GIN, GREAT FOOD
37 WATTON, BRECON, LD3 7EG

CHAPTERS RESTAURANT | SEASONALLY SET MENU
LION STREET, HAY-ON-WYE, HR3 5AA

THE TAI'R BULL INN | GREAT PUB FOOD
LIBANUS, BRECON, LD3 8EL

ALMOST GETTING LOST ON PEN Y FAN

Just a couple months before finishing this book, me and *'the lads'* decided we'd like to hike up Pen Y Fan. After becoming self-proclaimed mountain experts (which couldn't be further from the truth), we didn't want to take the usual *'motorway'* route up so we decided on an alternative which takes a very steep path up Corn Du before reaching Pen Y Fan. The weather was horrendous and visibility was at most 3-4 metres as we slogged our way up to the summit of Corn Du. From here, we didn't actually know which way to go to get to Pen Y Fan as the visibility was so poor and we didn't have a map or compass (rookie error). Fortunately, there was a guy who kindly pointed a couple of my mates in the correct direction, or so they thought. It wasn't until 30 minutes of descending that we realised we were heading in the complete opposite direction. For whatever reason, we were given the wrong directions from the chap at the top of Corn Du. After a quick stop to recalibrate ourselves, we managed to get back on the right track and eventually did reach Pen Y Fan. Once we returned to the car park we realised the guy who gave us the wrong directions was parked next to us in a foreign car and probably didn't understand our ask for directions. Rookies!

MY ITINERARY

DAY:		JOURNEY:	

ACTIVITIES	ACCOMMODATION

DAY:		JOURNEY:	

ACTIVITIES	ACCOMMODATION

DAY:		JOURNEY:	

ACTIVITIES	ACCOMMODATION

DAY:		JOURNEY:	

ACTIVITIES	ACCOMMODATION

MY ITINERARY

DAY: | **JOURNEY:**

ACTIVITIES	ACCOMMODATION

DAY: | **JOURNEY:**

ACTIVITIES	ACCOMMODATION

DAY: | **JOURNEY:**

ACTIVITIES	ACCOMMODATION

DAY: | **JOURNEY:**

ACTIVITIES	ACCOMMODATION

MY ITINERARY

DAY: | **JOURNEY:**

ACTIVITIES | **ACCOMMODATION**

DAY: | **JOURNEY:**

ACTIVITIES | **ACCOMMODATION**

DAY: | **JOURNEY:**

ACTIVITIES | **ACCOMMODATION**

DAY: | **JOURNEY:**

ACTIVITIES | **ACCOMMODATION**

MY ITINERARY

DAY: | **JOURNEY:**

ACTIVITIES	ACCOMMODATION

DAY: | **JOURNEY:**

ACTIVITIES	ACCOMMODATION

DAY: | **JOURNEY:**

ACTIVITIES	ACCOMMODATION

DAY: | **JOURNEY:**

ACTIVITIES	ACCOMMODATION

NOTES / JOURNAL

NOTES / JOURNAL

INDEX

INDEX

ROBBIE ROAMS
NO FUSS TRAVEL DOCUMENTARIES

WALES VIDEOS, TIPS & TOP 10 VIDEOS, WATCH NOW FOR FREE ON...

You Tube

THANK YOU FOR READING

I'd like to personally say thank you! I'm truly grateful that you have either purchased this book or received this book as a gift.

My number one priority when creating these travel guides is to help you have the best possible road trip, it's as simple as that.

The satisfaction I get from receiving messages and emails from you with stories from your trips is enormous! It really is! I can't stress how great it feels knowing that my book has helped somebody create special memories that will last a lifetime or even just inspired somebody to go on a road trip for the first time.

Now I may not know you personally, but, I do know we share the same curiosity for adventure, we share the same passion for experiencing new things and we definitely love seeing these beautiful locations! So with that said, I really hope your Welsh Road Trip is amazing, and, if you follow this book, there's a very high chance it's going to be!

Remember to keep me in the loop, I'd love to hear where you go and what you get up to on your trip. Please drop me a comment on YouTube, send me a message on Instagram or fire an email over to me. I will reply to literally any questions you may have about Wales or the book in general.

Thank you again and if we bump into each along the way, please stop and say hello!

Happy Road Tripping!

ROBBIE ROAMS

YOUTUBE - ROBBIE ROAMS | INSTAGRAM @ROBBIEROAMS
EMAIL - INFO@ROBBIEROAMS.COM

IN LOVING MEMORY

This book is dedicated to my Grandad - Francis Smith, who sadly passed away just a few days before I finished the last few pages. He was one of my biggest fans, an absolute gentleman and truly one of a kind! He was one of the reasons I have such an affinity with Wales. On Christmas day 2021, we had an instant photo taken together and I was absolutely gutted as I thought I'd lost it. It turns out the old git had it in his wallet the whole time! Rest easy Grandad, please send our love to Grandma and know that you will be missed by all of us!